Hawaiian Petroglyphs

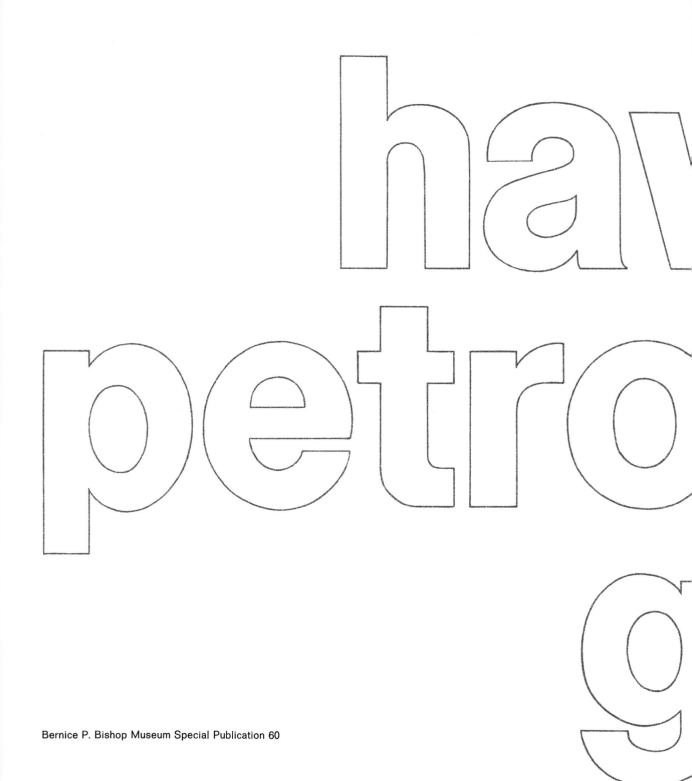

hawaii
petroglyphs

Bernice P. Bishop Museum Special Publication 60

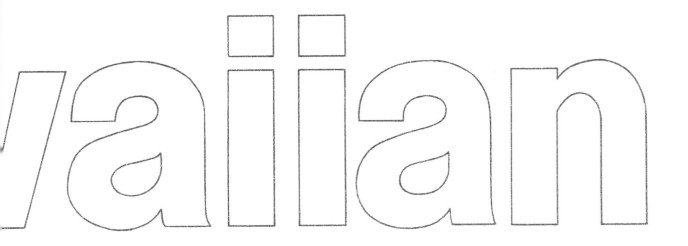

waiian

by J. Halley Cox with Edward Stasack

Bishop Museum Press, Honolulu, Hawaii

lyphs

Copyright © 1970 by Bishop Museum
1525 Bernice Street
Honolulu, Hawai'i 96817

Second printing 1977
Third printing 1980
Fourth printing 1985
Fifth printing 1988
Sixth printing 1990
Seventh printing 1995
Eighth printing 1999

ISBN 910240-09-4
Library of Congress Catalog Card No. 78-111491
Printed in Hong Kong

Designed by George Lenox

The first printing was made possible by a bequest
under the Will of the late Lani Booth, in memory of her
mother, Victoria Ward; and by a grant from the University
of Hawai'i Committee for the Preservation and Study of
Hawaiian Language, Art and Culture. The Board of
Directors of Bishop Museum is grateful to the Executor
of the Will of Lani Booth, and to the Committee for their
generous assistance.

Foreword

Professor J. Halley Cox at my urging undertook this presentation of Hawaiian petroglyphs, with the aid of Edward Stasack, his colleague in the Department of Art, University of Hawaii.

Mr. Cox participated in field trips sponsored jointly by Bishop Museum and the University of Hawaii, Manoa and Hilo Campus teams, when they were surveying the large petroglyph fields at Puako, Anaehoomalu, and Puuloa on the island of Hawaii between 1954 and 1960. He did much of the detailed mapping and recording. Because of this experience and his intimate knowledge of numerous other petroglyph areas throughout the islands, he is able to look upon them from the view of an archaeologist and ethnographer as well as of a professor of art. Mr. Stasack reinforces his thesis that petroglyphs are of significance as a universal artistic manifestation which, at the same time, helped to put man on the road to writing through the development of symbols. Both authors have a lively appreciation of the genius of the Hawaiians to depict, in a few bold lines, themselves, their animals, and meaningful objects in their culture.

Mr. Cox has brought together in these pages a complete listing of sites known presently to Bishop Museum, and an accurate and comprehensive general description of their petroglyphs. He tells how they were made, where they were made, and speculates rationally on when and why they were made on the basis of the clues offered by historical records, the surroundings, and the petroglyphs themselves. We are fortunate indeed that he has been willing to do this.

Kenneth P. Emory
Chairman, Department of Anthropology
Bernice P. Bishop Museum

Acknowledgments

To give full credit to each of the individuals who helped in a number of ways to bring this work to completion would be almost impossible. The authors are particularly grateful for kind assistance from the anthropology staff at Bernice Pauahi Bishop Museum, especially the encouragement of Dr. Kenneth P. Emory, and the help of Mr. Lloyd Soehren in running down maps, photos, many minor site details, and in general helping to keep the records straight. Mrs. Patience Bacon's assistance in typing the manuscript, and the graphic work on the site maps by Richard Rhodes are particularly appreciated. Assistant Professor William J. Bonk, University of Hawaii, Hilo Campus, and Mr. William K. Kikuchi are mainly responsible for the maps of the Puako and Puuloa sites that are reproduced from the Bishop Museum reports on these areas. For the many photographs that were used to develop the drawings, especially those from isolated sites on Hawaii, appreciation is extended to members of the archaeological surveys by the Bishop Museum, and especially to Mrs. Violet Hansen of Volcano, Hawaii.

Authorship of various parts of the manuscript is difficult to assign because of the extensive re-editing and the general give-and-take of ideas between the collaborators. Edward Stasack contributed a great deal of the materials in the chapters on "Sites" and "Techniques," and virtually all of the chapter on "Imagery and Symbolism." His extensive supply of photographs is the source for many of the illustrations. My own contribution, with much collaboration with Mr. Stasack and Dr. Emory, was in the other aspects of the subject: the petroglyphs in cultural context, history, and legend; the analysis of composition and the material concerning age and sequence; and the concluding statement about "Petroglyphs as Art." With the cooperation of the Bishop Museum Anthropology Department staff and the use of the Museum's records collected over many years, I was able to accomplish the routine compiling of the site list, bibliography, map locations, the illustrations, photo identifications, and captions.

In doing the illustrations I have used, wherever possible, a variety of styles as a means of suggesting the actual conditions of the forms, quality of stone surfaces, and the textures of the carving. The usually observable over-simplified or idealized line drawings do little more than suggest the general shapes and configuration and are subject to considerable inaccuracies of interpretation.

This note of acknowledgment is intended as an expression of gratitude and appreciation for assistance freely given by my colleagues and not as an avenue for disclaimer on any errors of fact, judgment, interpretation, or opinion that may be found here. These I must claim completely as my own.

J. H. C.

Contents

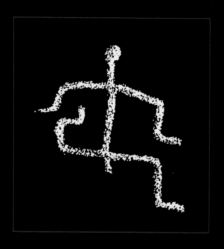

Introduction

In almost every part of the world where early man has lived he has made pictures by carving into natural rock surfaces. In a general way, all of these drawings, which are called petroglyphs, have a common character throughout the world, but it is also true that each culture has produced motifs and configurations within the limitations of the technique which are distinct enough to be recognized as area styles. The general common character and occasional similarities in detail between the petroglyphs in Hawaii and those occurring in other parts of the world—especially in Europe, North and South America, and India—have been used to suggest an actual common origin of the people who made them, or that communication existed between the cultures involved, no matter how far removed in time and space they may actually have been.

It is not surprising that much speculation as to the origins of the petroglyphs has occurred, since wherever they are found they always seem to lie just outside the area of easily explained phenomena. Almost nowhere in the world is there historic evidence relating to their origins. Even traditional histories and legends are generally lacking in useful clues. The present inhabitants of the various petroglyph areas throughout the world almost universally have no knowledge of who made them or why. Dating of petroglyphs would, of course, help solve some of the questions as to origin, but in most areas dating has been only tentative, being based upon secondary or indirect evidence. Hence, there is some mystery about petroglyphs, and this has stimulated considerable speculation and some misleading nonsense about them. As for the petroglyphs found in Hawaii, there is no reason whatever to suppose that they were not made by the immediate ancestors of the present Hawaiians in the not too distant past, without contacts with, or influence from other cultures.

The reasons for the similarities between petroglyph forms in various areas throughout the world lie in an interaction between two factors involved in their production. First, they are always a very simple and basic symbol, the form of which is limited by the need for forming an immediate and permanent image of the self or a spirit, or the making of a functioning symbol. This need may have a variety of origins, but it is nearly universal with man and, at its simplest level, produces similar forms. A statement by Giedion (1962), though based upon observations of paleolithic material in Europe, suggests the universal nature of basic symbols:

The reason symbols appeared so early, even before art, is owing to the workings of the human mind. Symbols were mankind's most effective weapons of survival when confronted by an inimical environment. In no other field was pre-historic man's imagination so abundant as in the invention of symbolic forms. Some of these will hold their secret forever, the signification of others is manifold. For the overwhelming majority, meaning revolves around an ardent desire for fertility and procreation. There are the hands and there are the circular forms: cuplike hollows in the rock in isolation or in association with animals or other objects; *ponctuations* (dots), forming their own patterns or surrounding other configurations; and perforations, as in the *bâtons de commandement* [pierced staves].

The second factor producing world-wide similarities is simply the technical limitations, since stone tools and rock surfaces are similar everywhere and limit the range of style.

In comparison with other Polynesians, Hawaiians were far more prolific in the production of petroglyphs. Some are found in almost every Polynesian area, some of them more elaborate and more expertly executed than those in Hawaii, but nowhere in the Pacific are there fields so extensive in size or so heavily covered with markings as those in the Hawaiian Islands, particularly on the island of Hawaii. These petroglyphs are a permanent record of an aspect of ancient Hawaii that will, with careful analysis, provide an added insight into that tradition. This record is unique in that the petroglyphs are not portable; they will forever remain in place if they are not disturbed by construction or vandalism. They can rarely be a part of a museum, and therefore their relationship to the landscape and to each other cannot be altered or put into false context, as so often happens to objects from past cultures when an attempt is made to save them. The illustrations

used here can only serve as a visual introduction to the subject of the Hawaiian petroglyphs and will indicate their general character and form. For a full appreciation of them they should be seen in the field where the impact of their orientation with the land, their extent, scale, the complex association between them, and the atmosphere of their existence can be fully experienced.

The Hawaiian petroglyphs are significant in a number of ways. As an aspect of the total culture of old Hawaii they serve as a supplementary source for the historian and archaeologist in reconstructing the culture. They have an intrinsic value which is aesthetic, or certainly a value beyond the mere implementation of concomitant studies in scientific areas. Petroglyphs can also reveal aspects of the nature of art; the motivations leading to the forming of symbols and images, the nature of the activity, and the kind of responses resulting from the contemplation of them. This aspect of the discussion is fostered by the conviction that the petroglyphs, in contrast to more sophisticated art forms—being devoid of elaborate technical processes, unconcerned with secondary associations, without literary or moral connotations—get directly to the prime content and meaning of art, to the roots of image making.

The location of any object has some effect on its appearance, meaning, and its expressive or emotional implications. One finds it almost impossible to really *see* an object only for what it is unless it is isolated or at least put into a neutral environment. A diamond amidst broken pieces of glass is nearly invisible, but shines brilliantly on black velvet. The influences of location go beyond just the visual implications and include all the senses. It is a fact that petroglyphs may be seen in more than one aspect, and that location contributes to the meaning, the sense of composition, and their expressive qualities.

The most obvious factor in the importance of location is that petroglyphs are not portable and will be seen in many cases in the same environment in which they were created. This is significant because substantially the same physical conditions will be affecting the viewer as affected the petroglyph maker. There are, of course, exceptions where recent plant growth has established a very different environment, and where extremely different weather might influence the mood of the viewer. However, even weather in Hawaii is fairly constant as long as the trade winds blow; and there is little seasonal change. Even natural erosion and weathering have a lesser effect on the images than one would at first imagine, since both the petroglyph and the surrounding rock surfaces are affected equally by wind, rain, sun, and time. Therefore, the relationship of the petroglyph to the surface into which it was pecked probably was little affected through the years by changes of color, texture, or harmony. This would inhibit changes in meaning caused by more or less accidental associations unintended by the maker, and perhaps tend also to mellow but not to change the expressive implications of petroglyph imagery.

The following is an excerpt from a letter from one of the authors written about a hike to Pohue Bay from a camping place near South Point (Ka Lae), Hawaii.

The last day of the six we spent at this site I traveled about sixteen miles total on the rugged coastline in a nearly disastrous misadventure that ended with a searching party that found me on

ig. 1. A small section of the Puako site (HA-E3-1)* in the aeo Trail area showing the domed *pahoehoe* surface broken nto separate sheets. This particular surface is not very hard and rosion is noticeable (the darkened sections). Much of this site as covered with *kiawe* trees as in the background here, until was excavated in 1955. See page 28 and Figure 38.

B. P. Bishop Museum site numbers.

the point of exhaustion. My feet were so badly blistered that I walked with a limp for two weeks.

In some ways the experience was nearly a mystical one. The area, Pohue Bay, is almost totally inaccessible and certainly no one has lived there for many, many years. There were occasional wells of brackish water which, when my water supply ran out, I drank without regard for possible contamination. These wells contained scattered bones of wild goats and pigs. Under normal conditions they would not be considered for drinking purposes. But I lived. The coastline is dramatic with alternating strips of lava rock (from ancient eruptions up the slope to Mauna Loa) and the natural terrain, a fairly continuous line of cliffs anywhere from ten to fifty feet above the water. The entire area is barren.

With the proper training one is able to follow the ancient Hawaiian trail to Pohue Bay. My training was slight and several times I became lost among high, magnificently ragged and tortured rocks. The sound of the sea was always there to give a sense of direction but without the trail one was continually baffled by blind alleys. It was impossible not to suffer from frustration and anxiety . . . and then a tremendous relief when the worn rock surfaces, or a white coral trail marker amidst the unending brown and gray showed the trail again.

Each time I "sensed" the presence of the trail I was sincerely moved by the imagery that it automatically brought to mind. Seeing it was not the thing . . . it was the physical act of being on it. I have been in other sacred areas, seen other ancient and historical sites, but this feeling was special and fortunate. Being alone and in a precarious situation was obviously part of it. One becomes necessarily interested in basic things. The excitement of discovery and the physical danger cause a keenness of perception and a very real consciousness. One is fully and truly conscious. All this, of course, before I was physically exhausted. There was no time for meditation, no interest in profundities. At each rest there was the usual dichotomy of a great awareness of self and still a positive and complete identification with the place.

The walk to Pohue Bay took nearly six and a half hours. It was small and there were only four coconut palms, a welcome green. At one time there must have been a well or a spring but it was covered by a lava flow that sliced the bay in half. Only after you were in it did you realize that everywhere there were petroglyphs. I must have passed forty or fifty before I realized they were there. Time has made them a part of the land. They are usually found in clusters and whatever the reason for the choice of site, one is aware that there are as many good sites unworked.

The big view of the area is of a long and gradual slope that moves up to the top of Mauna Loa, 13,000 feet, but so very gradual that the mountain is a hill, a rise, impossible to be tolerated as a high mountain. Unbelievable, the total mass of this mountain from its base is greater than that of the entire Sierra Nevadas. A softly colored sand beach and a few deteriorated rocks marking house sites a short distance from the water are convincing of the once present inhabitants. There are two potato shaped hills nearby, one hollow and containing a few petroglyph It is very quiet. Even the constant wind, with no trees to affect, is silent.

Interestingly, there was no feeling of peace or calm. In this broad area with no signs of currency there was an almost threatening climate. Once before when I stayed out alone in the desolation of Anaehoomalu it was much the same. Despite a grea weariness, and again, blistered feet, I was unable to sleep through the night because of this same feeling. Now, I am not convinced of spirits, although most people here are, but when I talked of my solitary adventure at Anaehoomalu I was told that n Hawaiian would ever have gone where I did alone and at night.

One would probably imagine Hawaii to have much more sand, palm trees, and clear lagoons than expanses of barren country such as that described in the above, and it is for this reason that a description of the kind of setting most commonly found for petroglyphs is important. It is not what one expects and it would be misleading to visualize them in any other way. Certainly, there are petroglyphs found in some of the more glamorous locations, but the main fields at Anaehoomalu, Paniau, and Puuloa are all similar to the terrain on the way to and at Pohue Bay.

Just off busy Nuuanu Avenue in Honolulu, a few feet from the road encircling the Honolulu Memorial Park, an outcropping of large boulders forms a prominence above Nuuanu Stream. It is not too difficult to clamber down, over and between the boulders, to see the petroglyphs there. There are beautifully drawn dogs with perky ears cocked forward and graceful tails sweeping up and back; also refined images of men—or more likely chiefs or spirits of men—judging from the "rainbow" arches from shoulder to shoulder over their heads. The pictures continue into the shadowy crevices and narrow passages between the rocks, in some places almost too narrow or low for access. In the days before the rank growth of the *haole koa* trees this spot would have been a distinct landmark on the trail along the right bank of the stream.

A bit farther upstream the canyon narrows and the well-used path follows the base of the low cliffs at the water's edge. A number of other petroglyphs can be found on this cliff face before reaching Kapena Falls, not more than a half mile up the stream from the main group. These, however, are not as finely made or as varied, being mostly groups of simple lineal figures. In contrast to Pohue Bay, with a landscape about as isolated and forbidding as is conceivable, the Nuuanu petroglyphs are at our back door, on the edge of a pleasant wooded stream bed, and they are about as fine an example of the art as can be found.

As the distribution maps (pages 80–96) indicate, petroglyph sites are widespread in the islands, having been reported on all except Kahoolawe. New sites are occasionally reported, but such discoveries are usually small, isolated occurrences and it is doubtful whether any major finds will be made that will add significantly to our present knowledge. The number of petroglyph sites roughly reflects the population of the islands in ancient times. A census count was not taken until long after the 1778 discovery of the Hawaiian Islands, but from reports of early voyagers, estimates have been made for population of the various islands. An early population estimate made by Jarves (from Schmitt, 1965, p. 200) is compared in the following table to the number of sites and petroglyphs on the islands.

	Population Estimate	Petroglyphs	
Island	Jarves 1823	Sites	Units
Hawaii	85,000	±70	±22,600
Maui	20,000	18	450
Lanai	2,500	23	760
Molokai	3,500	5	500
Oahu	20,000	9	150
Kauai	10,000	9	220
Niihau	1,000	1	1
Kahoolawe	50	0	—
Total	142,050	±135	±24,681

The occurrence of petroglyphs is almost entirely limited to the dry sides of the islands and generally to open country near the shore, the dry leeward areas being preferred for habitation by the Hawaiians. The sites are seldom within the small village centers but are on or near the trails between habitation sites. There seems to be no particular consistency in location in relation to fresh water or other geographical features, as is sometimes the case where petroglyphs are found in other parts of the world. That fewer sites have been found on the wet sides of the islands is probably owing at least in part to the density of vegetation. However, sites as large as the major fields on Hawaii would not easily remain undiscovered.

As an indication of the size and importance of the various sites, estimates of the number of petroglyph units at each site is given in the site list (page 81). For a number of reasons units can seldom be counted with any accuracy, as a glance at Figure 37 will indicate. Configurations do not give much of a clue as to which mark goes with which, or which ones can be read as individual units. Any count is merely a generalization, indicating concentration. This limitation tends to reduce the value of purely statistical studies of these sites unless intensive examination is made *in situ*. Since each site is also characterized by the kind of surface on which the petroglyphs are made, some discussion of these surfaces seems in order. There are five such surface types: *pahoehoe*, waterworn boulders, cliff faces, cave walls, and sandstone beach shelves.

Fields of billowy *pahoehoe* lava flows account for the majority of the sites on the island of Hawaii, including the three major sites, Puako, Anaehoomalu, and Puuloa. *Pahoehoe* is formed by a highly viscous lava flow that has cooled while spreading across a fairly flat area. In cooling it bulges slightly into low billowy mounds which crack apart at their edges forming slightly curved surfaces 4 to 10 feet across (Fig. 1). The surface tends to harden into a glaze which resists erosion. When broken by the petroglyph maker, the exposed granular interior contrasts with the undisturbed surface. Petroglyphs on these surfaces tend to show up very well, as they were easily

Fig. 2. Part of a line of men at the Puako site (HA-E3-1) in the Paniau area, an excellent example of the triangular body type. Note the "child" under the arm of the top figure. This area is notable for its numerous family-like groups and rows of figures.

Fig. 3 and Fig. 4. The glazed *pahoehoe* at Kamooalii (HV-210) is coarse and granular underneath resulting in images that are ragged and highly textured.

Fig. 5. A typical boulder site. This one is at Kukui Point on Lanai (LA-209).

made to an inch or so in depth (Fig. 2). However, some tend to erode by the crumbling of the sharp edge of the glaze, which disrupts the clarity of the images (Figs. 3, 4).

Some of these *pahoehoe* flows continue uninterrupted for miles, offering unlimited surfaces for the carvers. This raises the question, to be discussed later, of why particular areas were chosen for the pictures. Since erosion was at a minimum on the *pahoehoe* flows, there was little vegetation on them in the dry areas in ancient times. At present, however, the introduced *kiawe* (algaroba) tree has become established in some places, as at the Puako site in South Kohala, making it necessary to clear the trees and accumulated debris in order to find the petroglyphs.

Rounded large boulders, and the flatter split faces of these, are the second most favored surface used by the petroglyph artists (Fig. 5). Carvings are found on boulders ranging in size from 2 feet to 15 feet in diameter. Generally, these boulders are harder throughout than the *pahoehoe* and have a patinated surface that is slightly different in color from the stone immediately beneath the surface. The petroglyphs on these surfaces are generally not as deeply carved as those on *pahoehoe*, usually not more than $\frac{1}{8}$ of an inch. The resisting surface requires a somewhat more refined technique. With age, some of the shallow figures become very difficult to see because the exposed surfaces slowly discolor to match the surface of the boulder. The area on a boulder is finite, limiting the number of figures that it may contain. In this aspect it differs from the *pahoehoe*, in that the limited surface tends to determine the boundaries of a site. The usable surfaces of the boulders on the hillside at Luahiwa, Lanai, are pretty well covered with petroglyphs, and one has a feeling that if there had been additional boulders there would have been more petroglyphs. Most of the other sites on Lanai are also boulder sites, as are those at Moanalua, Oahu; Maalaea, Maui; and Wailua, Kauai. Although these boulders are usually much too large to be portable, a few petroglyphs are found on stones that have been transported and set into *heiau* walls. There are examples

of this at Kaunolu and at Kahea, Lanai; at Punaluu spring in Puna, Hawaii; Kamooalii *heiau*, Kau, Hawaii; and on a fishing *heiau* at South Point, Hawaii. They no doubt had some function relating to the sacredness of the structure, and therefore were taboo.

Vertical cliff surfaces offer a surface similar to the boulders, but are usually somewhat finer in texture, and more compact. Petroglyphs on cliff walls are found at the Nuuanu Valley sites on Oahu (Fig. 6). Most of the sites on Maui are on cliffs (Fig. 7). If the cliffs are quite ancient or exposed to moisture, the surfaces have a patina that can be knocked away by bruising, which tends to produce broad, unformalized, rough-edged images. Clearly define edges and very delicate forms are sometimes found on the cliff faces. These were made by incising with a sharp tool.

Fig. 6.   Dogs and men at the Nuuanu Valley site (OA-A5-1) in Honolulu. These are on large boulders forming a number of narrow passages in which the petroglyphs were made. In contrast to the usual lineal forms, these are pecked out across the surface of the figure and the edges are carefully delineated by grinding.

At least two other types of surfaces were used, the each shelves and cave walls. The beach shelf is usually a waterworn *pahoehoe* or of sandstone (calcareous ck), as at Keoneloa, Kauai (Fig. 8). The water levels have parently changed slightly at Keoneloa and also possibly Anaehoomalu and Kahaluu, Hawaii, and the Keaau and upukea sites on Oahu, so that these beach-shelf sites e now under water at high tide and often covered ith sand.

Fig. 8. Petroglyphs at Keoneloa Beach, Kauai (KA-B2-1). These are on a limestone ledge that is almost always covered with a deep layer of sand. The water level has undoubtedly changed since the pictures were made. In almost all of the figures at this site the technique by which they were made is clearly evident— rubbing with a sharp pointed instrument forming a straight smooth line terminating in a tapering point.

ig. 7. A view of the cliff face at Olowalu, Maui (MA-D2-2). The urface is very compact so that the carvings are shallow and isible only as a discoloration. These have been chalked for hotographing. The design above the top right figure is a anoe sail.

ig. 9. Figures cut into the limestone beach shelf at Pupukea,)ahu (OA-F1-9). These petroglyphs can rarely be seen since ney are usually under several inches of sand.

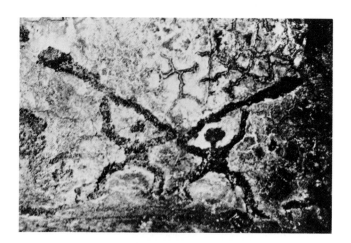

Fig. 10.   A pair of "paddle dancers" or possibly two men fighting with clubs, on a cave wall at Apua, Puna (HV-185). The wall is white on the surface and dark below, making a striking contrast. The action suggested in this composition is unusual, although mirror-imagery is not uncommon in the Hawaiian petroglyphs.

Fig. 12.   Figures and symbols in a cave near Pahala, Kau, Hawaii (HA-B7-1) showing the crusty white surface which has been broken away to form the images. The two central figures have specialized head forms. At the right is an unusual profile figure with arms outstretched.

Fig. 11.   Petroglyphs outlined in chalk on a cave wall at Keauhou, Kau (HV-76).

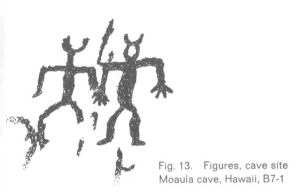

Fig. 13.   Figures, cave site
Moaula cave, Hawaii, B7-1

However, there is no evidence that the petroglyphs found in caves are directly associated with these functions. It is also self-evident that they were not placed in caves for reasons of secrecy, magic hunting ritual, or fertility, as were many of the paleolithic cave paintings of Europe. At most of the cave sites the petroglyphs are near the entrances, as though they were a kind of signal to the passer-by indicating shelter. In one, however, a sense of mystery is imparted by a group of petroglyphs in the pitch-black, narrow tunnel in the interior of "turtle cave" near Pahala, Hawaii. The name comes from a small, smooth, rounded dome of lava, like the shell of a turtle, that protrudes from the floor of the cave. The elliptical dome, about two feet long is a hardened bubble, which formed an island in the river of fluid lava. It is crowded with simple, crude lineal figures and a few odd marks that unfortunately reveal nothing of their possible mystic origins.

In general each individual site is characterized by the use of only one of these surface types, even if a variety of surfaces are available. The making of petroglyphs was not stimulated merely by the suitability or availability of the rock surfaces—too many suitable places have no petroglyphs to allow for this—but because the place had some cultural significance. It is therefore useful to examine the site areas and the kind of petroglyphs on them, in the context of pertinent culture patterns, for clues to the reasons for the choice of the site and the function of the pictures. It is evident that some of the petroglyphs had their origin in magic and traditional rites, although the nature of these activities is known for only a couple of the sites. No doubt they were made for different reasons in different places, and probably were part of formal observances of various kinds. In general, it appears that the force behind the creation of the petroglyphs was the need for visual images and symbols related to the following: (1) Recording of trips and communication concerning other events, on trails and at boundaries; (2) A concern for insuring long life and personal well being; and (3) The commemoration of events and legends.

Considering the great number of caves, literally hundreds, in the islands, many of which show evidence of some kind of use in the past, it is surprising that only a few lava-tube cave petroglyph sites are recorded and, with few exceptions, all are located in the district of Kau, Hawaii. The lava tubes were formed by the cooling from the outside around the core of a highly fluid river of lava. As the fluid core flows out the lower end, a hollow tube remains. Some of these lava-tube caves run for miles just a few feet under the surface. The walls of these caves usually have a glazed, brittle surface like the *pahoehoe.* The petroglyphs were made by breaking the surface and chipping into the darker stone beneath. If this undersurface is soft, the images are apt to be rough-edged and irregular, since the stone will crumble easily under the action of the tool. The technique and appearance of these petroglyphs is essentially similar to the coarser *pahoehoe* types. Because of the usually whitish plaster-like surface, the dark petroglyphs contrast strongly with it even in the dim light of torches. Some lava-tube caves were used in ancient times as temporary shelters, or places of refuge in times of war, and others were used as burial places.

Fig. 14. Many of the forms that surround the Puuloa mound are enigmatic but at the same time bold and clearly structured, which suggests that the designer had a purpose and was in control of the shape rather than following a random whim. In numbers, dots and circles still predominate.

The Petroglyph in Cultural Context

Any attempt to discuss the nature of the Hawaiian
petroglyphs, the technique, subject matter or meanings,
or to define the forces that caused their creation, should
take into account the nature of ancient Hawaiian life.
It is not advisable here to attempt an extensive recounting
of the cultural background. These features will be briefly
related in context with the discussion of the various
aspects of the petroglyph art. One characteristic that
should not be overlooked is that of the unity of cultural
patterns in Hawaiian life. In highly advanced civilizations
activities are segmented by specialization; life becomes
a collection of separate activity areas such as politics,
religion, economics, art, education, and the like. In the
Hawaiian realm the distinction between such separate
entities was tenuous; they were instead fused into a way
of life. With a close integration between all aspects of
life what may seem to be a religious ritual or an act of
magic could as well be described as a custom, a practical
necessity, or a useful technique. The student of the
Hawaiian petroglyphs must face this equivocality, since

Fig. 15. A group of petroglyphs at Kamooalii (HV-210) seemingly
composed around the central figure which is suggestive of a
protective or encompassing gesture.

many of the various types seem to reflect actions, intentions, and meanings on several levels at once.

As more petroglyphs were discovered and recorded and information about them became available, some factors appeared which have significance in the attempt to relate them to the life of the ancient Hawaiians. This is not to say that the relationships can be stated as proven facts. Many of these raise as many questions as they may answer. A brief preview of some of these more noticeable relationships will serve to indicate the direction of some of the investigations (and speculations) and will suggest the various aspects of the cultural pattern with which the petroglyphs are connected.

Means of transportation. Although by far the most numerous images are human figures, dots, and circles, there are a number of representations of canoes, canoe paddles, and sails, alone, in various combinations, and associated with human figures. There are also artificial footprints and, in a few instances, lines of men apparently on the march (Fig. 61). In the historic period sailing ships and men on horses were depicted. Many of these forms, including some of the dots and circles, seem quite clearly to be marks left by travelers, often including the mode of travel.

The family. In representations of the human figure there is often a clear distinction between sexes. When these occur in groups, with smaller human figures associated or attached, the suggestion of families is unavoidable. Some even appear to be birth scenes. There are also female figures with smaller figures within the torso representing pregnancy (Fig. 64).

The supernatural. Although discernible only by inference, some of the human figure forms suggest supernatural beings, especially those with fantastic heads or headdresses. There are figures with heads like birds with outstretched wings, bird-like profiles, unnatural head forms with upright bars, dots, circles, and loops, and figures with arches over the head. These may be representations of *'aumakua.* Each family group, and each individual, had a special *'aumakua,* or ancestral guardian

Fig. 16. Double canoe
Kalailinui, Maui, B22-2

Fig. 17. Ship
Kapalaoa, Hawaii, D24-6

Fig. 18. Horse and rider
Anaehoomalu, Hawaii, E1-1

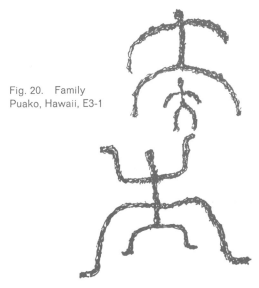

Fig. 19. Family
Puako, Hawaii, E3-1 (Kaeo trail)

Fig. 20. Family
Puako, Hawaii, E3-1

Fig. 21. A complex but neatly designed image at Pohue Bay
(HA-B23-40) which has indications of being added to at
successive stages. This might possibly be another symbolization
of a birth scene.

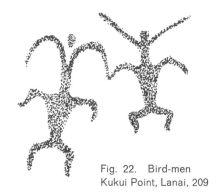

Fig. 22. Bird-men
Kukui Point, Lanai, 209

god, to which offerings were made and rituals were directed. Since the source of an individual's *mana* lay in the *'aumakua*, no significant activity was undertaken without proper action in its regard. A second possibility is that these unnatural human forms may be representations of the *akua*, the major gods. The head elaborations are similar in idea to those developed in the wooden images of the *akua*, particularly in the portable stick images and the large temple images. Possibly they may represent the *ali'i* (nobility) who were considered to be direct descendants of the *akua*, and were therefore sacred. In this context the head designs might be symbols for the excessive *mana* of the *ali'i*, or possibly a means of suggesting the crested and spiked feather helmet, which was a striking element of ceremonial dress limited to the *ali'i*. Another supernatural symbol may be represented in the apparently incomplete human figures. Those with a vertical body line and a cross bar describe rather accurately the wooden image of Lono, the god carried during tax collecting and used in the *makahiki* festival which followed. (See pages 32–33.)

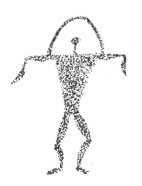

Fig. 23. Figure, rainbow
Nuuanu, Oahu, A5-1

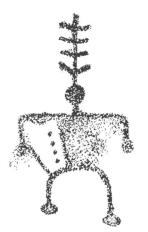

Fig. 24. Figure with headdress
Kaupulehu, Hawaii, D22-19

Fig. 25. Figure with headcrest
Kaupulehu, Hawaii, D22-19

Some of the animal representations might be symbols or supernatural spirits. Similar to the 'aumakua was another class of protective spirits, the 'unihipili, which was often centered in an animal form, at times a pet or a specific individual wild bird, fish, or shark. These personal protective spirits were created by the deification of a deceased member of the family whose spirit was released into the animal. The act of transfer was done by a *kahuna,* a specialist who was gifted and trained in this activity. The most common occurrences among the animal petroglyphs are dogs, birds, turtles, and chickens, but even these are rare in comparison to the number of human figures. Any of these may be symbols for protective spirits, but of course dogs or chickens may simply represent these animals with their owners. Surprisingly, the most common 'aumakua or 'unihipili animal was the shark, which does not occur in a clearly discernible form in the known petroglyphs, although at Oluwalu, Maui, there is a well-drawn whale.

Repetitive symbols. Within the nonfigurative types of petroglyphs a number of the simpler elements sometimes

Fig. 28.   Dog, chicken, chicken, turtle
Puako, Hawaii, E3-1

Fig. 27.   Dog and birds
Kukui Point, Lanai, 209

Fig. 26.   Lono symbols
Puako, Hawaii, E3-1 (Kaeo trail)

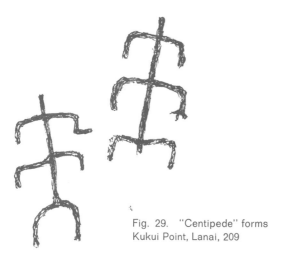

Fig. 29.   "Centipede" forms
Kukui Point, Lanai, 209

Fig. 30.   Symbol
Puuloa, Hawaii, HV-225

occur in groups. Dots, bars, and circles are found in various configurations such as rows, circles, or concentric relationships, confined within boundaries. At times these are connected to or associated with human figures. At one site complete human figures are repeated in rows (Fig. 61) and there are a number of examples of figures with multiple limbs. The meanings of these assemblies depend, of course, on the meaning of the individual symbol, which may be an event, a person, an object, or possibly an abstract idea. The group can then be a record, a tally, a score, a collection, a census, a mnemonic device, or possibly even a directive. Since most of these repetitive marks are not drawings of the objects they symbolize, it is impossible to know the meanings of the relationships without some "inside" information. Fortunately, in two cases some information on them has been obtained from Hawaiian informants. One of these refers to the recording of a number of persons in a traveling party and to numbers of trips. The other account reveals the possible use of a kind of tally system for births and family groups.

   Concentrations.   Hawaiian petroglyphs are usually found in groups, rather than as single isolated units. There is some limited patterning to the position and to the characteristics of the sites where the clustering occurs. That these patterns would be related to cultural factors is a foregone conclusion, but the nature of the relationship is not always clear. Almost all sites are near the shore. They occur generally along known trails. Some are near ancient land boundaries. Some sites are at what might have been rest areas where some shelter is available—caves, overhangs, or depressions. Still others are on lava prominences or boulder outcroppings that are in contrast to the immediate surroundings.

   There may have been no true "choice" of the sites, but certain areas may have become favored places for the making of petroglyphs merely by accident, convenience, and custom. However, since petroglyphs are obviously not just casual or trivial doodles, and many of them appear to have a structured meaning in the culture, fuller explanation of the "site choice" is needed. Religious dictates, magic and secret formulae, ritual considerations of *mana*, and conditions of *kapu*—in other words supernatural forces—along with others more mundane entered into the choice of temple sites, house sites and positions, burial areas, garden plots, and probably into every act that in any way altered the landscape. Some such decisions were certainly more critical and involved than others, but the petroglyph maker, too, was likely to be guided partly by these forces and would have been concerned with the consequence of an unsuitable choice. The petroglyphs have ties with ancient Hawaiian culture on all levels and, since these ties are numerous and interlocked, none can be seen clearly, and certainly no single relationship should be regarded as the only one of consequence in an explanation.

Information about the most concentrated complex of petroglyphs in Hawaii, a small lava hill in the district of Puna, Hawaii, called Puuloa, reveals the magic and symbolic nature of at least some of the petroglyphs. It also shows that the site itself had special significance that imparted magic or *mana* to the ritual performed on its surface. Though much is still unknown about it, because of the importance of this site further reference will be made to it in other parts of this study.

The hill, a *pahoehoe* dome, is not a dominant feature of this very extensive lava flow, being only a little higher than the neighboring hills. Shelter is available in a nearby depression, a collapsed lava bubble where it is possible to get out of the sun, rain, or wind. There is no water and little vegetation except grass and a few widely scattered *'ohi'a* trees. The hill is about a mile from the shore and the trail from the south turns inland from the coastal village site of Kealakomo, apparently for no other reason than to reach Puuloa. In this case it is probable that the trail is a result of the significance of the place rather than that the petroglyph site occurs there because of the trail.

Fig. 31. Circles
Milolii, Hawaii, C5-1

Fig. 32.   The surface on top of the *pahoehoe* mound at Puuloa
(HV-225) is carved into a textured dome with thousands of
cup-like depressions, circles and bars. There are no figurative
elements in this area. The erosion of the surface is no doubt
hastened by the crowding and overlapping of the symbols. The
largest circles are about 8 inches in diameter.

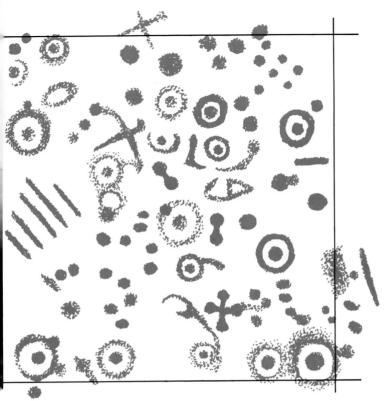

Fig. 33.   Symbols in a five-foot square
Puuloa, Hawaii, HV-225

The literal meaning of Puuloa is "long hill" (*pu'u:* hill, *loa:* long), but the Hawaiians of Kalapana (the nearest inhabitants today) interpret it as "Hill of Long Life" and associate the magic of the name with the function of the petroglyphs there. The *pahoehoe* dome and much of the surrounding surface is covered with thousands of petroglyphs, those on top of the hill being mostly simple, round, cup-like holes pecked into the lava. There is testimony that it was the custom for Hawaiians to come to Puuloa with the *piko** of a new-born child, make a hole here, place the *piko* in it, and cover the hole with a stone. If the *piko* remained overnight (or disappeared—there is conflicting evidence about which would be effective) long life would be assured for the child. The practice of special disposal of the umbilical cord for protective

Piko is used to describe both the umbilical stump and the umbilical cord. It has not been made clear which is buried in this ceremony, but it is assumed it is the stump because of its smaller size. See footnote, page 69.

Fig. 34. Dots, circles, symbols
Various sites

reasons is a widespread practice and the Hawaiians use
other means of such disposal in other areas.

Other petroglyph forms are found at Puuloa, including
human figures, elaborations on the holes, dots, circles,
and lines, groups and rows of these (family groups), all
probably concerned with birth and life. If the holes are
containers for the *piko*, the dots and simpler forms are
probably symbols for the container or symbols for the
piko. The repeated units are symbols for groups, a *piko-*
tally, or the number in the family.

At Puuloa there was apparently a special aura of
mana, associated with the hill and its name, localized on
the summit of the rise. The ceremony of making the
petroglyphs, continuing through successive generations,
increased the magic of the site. No other sites are known
where petroglyphs function in just this way, but other
meanings and functions can be assumed as probable.
Some, as at Puuloa, may relate to protective magic,
some to other human needs.

If the activities related to the spiritual realm were
responsible for some of the petroglyphs, the more practi
cal aspects of day-to-day existence—fishing, gardening,
communication, travel, taxes, amusements, social contro
and the like—though never devoid of spiritual connotations, must have also been a stimulus for their creation.
However, the precise nature of these more mundane
relationships can only be surmised. As stated earlier, the
petroglyphs reflect a population factor, most of the sites
being near the shore on the trails between the habitation
sites. In ancient times almost the entire population
resided on the coast, not in village centers but in family
dwelling sites scattered along the shore. There was some
clustering of houses in the areas of higher productivity ar
at the residences of the chiefs. This residence pattern
required trails near the shore which normally circled
the island, as well as trails from the shore to upland
areas. The island was divided into wedge-shaped district
with boundaries running from the shore to the mountain
tops. Each district was a complete, politically autonomou

nd economically self-sufficient unit under the feudal ontrol of a high chief.

ach large district was again cut into smaller sections known as hupua'as. The name was derived from the ahu or altar which was rected at the district boundary line and on which the yearly ayments were made at the time of Makahiki. On this altar was lso placed the small image of a pig or pua'a. . . . A typical hupua'a was a long narrow strip running from the sea to the ountain. . . .

    People living in one ahupua'a had a right to use what grew ere. They could go to the mountains for timber. They could ather pili grass and olona. They could fish in the waters off their istrict. . . . No person could cross the boundaries of his ahupua'a take anything. This being the case, it was important that the oundaries be well known. . . . (Wise, 1965, p. 84)

This source and others suggest that the *kapu* controls n trespass stipulated that passing over a boundary could ake place only on an established foot trail and most kely on only one such trail. Russell A. Apple (1965, p. 65) n his Appendix 2 describes his type "A" (oldest) rails as follows:

    a. Single-file foot trails, characterized by many turnings and ne-man width. If on coast, persistently following configurations f shore line where passable, skirting inland around major land bstacles, such as cliffs (*thus there was a single beach trail round most of the island*) [italics supplied].
    b. Coast-inland trails within each *ahupua'a* of this type [not rossing boundaries].
    c. Taboo areas [were] not crossed by such trails.
    d. Over soil: a recognizable trace, some places deep.
    e. Over "clinker" lava (aa): steppingstones, usually of smooth, aterworn stones (*'ala*).
    f. Over "billowy" lava (pahoehoe): usually no trace (followed asiest and shortest route); some cracks filled with small stones; ome low spots with causeways of rocks (*kipaepae*); stepping-tones of angular-edged rocks. Occasional piles of rocks to mark rails; perhaps petroglyphs also. . . .

This seems to describe a shore or beach trail and uggests it as the only route of travel between *ahupua'a* nd districts. There are enough occurrences of similar ypes of trails some distance inland from the shore within 1/4 mile), and some several miles inland also

encircling the island, to suggest that more than one trail actually existed. The beach route was for fishermen and access along the *ahupua'a* shore line, while the main route for travelers was the coastal or upper trail which skirted dwellings, shore *heiau,* and *kapu* areas. This upper trail afforded *kapu*-free crossing of boundaries of the *ahupua'a* and across district boundaries such as during the *makahiki* processions, or for a chief's retinue when traveling between districts. On the island of Hawaii it is along these upper coastal trails that most of the petroglyph sites that relate to trails are to be found.

    When traveling by foot, distances between settlements might be several hours apart, particularly across the barren, sparsely settled lava "deserts" of the island of Hawaii, such as are found in North Kona, South Kohala, and the entire coastal area of Kau and South Puna. Discomforts of travel are mainly the heat and rough terrain but respite from wind and occasional rain would also be welcome. Rest areas might be collapsed lava bubbles or other depressions, caves, cliff shelters, a grove of trees, or at an occasional brackish water well. If the surrounding areas are suitable, petroglyphs are likely to be found at such places.

    After the first one or two pictures were made by passing travelers, others might have been made simply from the stimulation of the existing example—by sugges-tion. In time the making of the petroglyphs at the rest site could have become a custom or even a magic action, required for luck, well-being, or safety. In this view the reasons for creating the first petroglyphs at the site may be immaterial; rather, the meanings and reasons grew out of or became attached to the continued activity.

    Possibly the important site at Anaehoomalu had its origins in this manner. The petroglyph forms here suggest no definite scheme or function. They are greatly varied, with human figures of all kinds, dots, circles, and abstract shapes sometimes overlying each other. This site is in a large depression at the end of a rough stretch of trail over an *aa* lava flow. There are shelter caves and a brackish water well near the shore. A number of other

Fig. 36.   A small section of the very extensive Anaehoomalu site (HA-E1-1) which has a wide variety of forms, many of considerable complexity. Large enclosures are often used to encompass smaller elements in what is apparently a means of giving them a special presentation by isolating them from the common ground.

Fig. 35.   A general view of the *pahoehoe* flow at Kamooalii (HV-210). Many of the petroglyph sites are found in similar barren terrain. This is one of the few large sites that is not near the shore. It is in the vicinity of a *heiau* in the Kau desert approximately 2½ miles inland at an elevation of about 1,000 feet.

sites, such as those at Pohue Bay, Halape, Kaupulehu, Miloli, Naalehu on the island of Hawaii, and possibly several of the cave sites, may also have originated as rest-areas.

The important Puako complex, however, like the Puuloa site, does not seem to be a natural rest spot and probably had some other special quality that attracted the petroglyph makers. It should be noted also that each of these two areas has its own type of imagery and in the concentrated center of each the petroglyph type is restricted almost entirely to one form. This suggests that the earliest carvers resorted to a specific pattern for a specific function. At Puuloa (Fig. 37) the purpose was the disposal of the *piko*. At Puako (Fig. 38), where there is a predominance of simple lineal figures depicting family groups and birth scenes, the site may have functioned in some way relating to birth.

Petroglyphs on trails may have still other origins and functions. They may have some connection with the *makahiki* activities. It was at the boundaries of the *ahupua'a* on the coastal trails that the pig-altars for the *makahiki* ceremony were located. Some petroglyphs that are near the boundaries served to indicate to the traveler that another *ahupua'a* or district was beginning at this point. In other words they may mark the boundary as well as marking the trail. The crossing of some boundaries may have "required" the making of a petroglyph by the traveler. The ritual would be similar in meaning to many such acts that are known to have been the normal pattern in ancient Hawaii. A good example is described by Ellis (1842, Vol. 4, p. 15):

Within a few yards of the upper edge of the pass, under the shade of surrounding bushes and trees, two rude and shapeless stone idols are fixed, one on each side of the path, which the natives call *Akua no ka Pari*, gods of the precipice; they are usually covered with pieces of white tapa, native cloth; and every native who passes by to the precipice, if he intends to descend, lays a green bough before these idols, encircles them with a garland of flowers, or wraps a piece of tapa around them, to render them propitious to his descent; all who ascend from the opposite side make a similar acknowledgment for the supposed

protection of the deities, whom they imagine to preside over the fearful pass.

By no means all boundaries are marked by petroglyphs and many petroglyphs do occur in patterns that seem unrelated to trails and boundaries; but it should be remembered that some of the present property lines may not be ancient boundaries, even though the names of *ahupua'a* and districts are ancient, and that in many areas the ancient trails are now not visible.

Both the Anaehoomalu and Puako sites are near the boundary between North Kona and South Kohala. There is a small group of petroglyphs at Kaulanamauna near the line between the districts of South Kona and Kau. On the southeast coast there are minor sites near the boundary of Kau and Puna and a significantly larger one at the village of Kealakomo 3 miles east of the present boundary. Another group is at Halape 2 miles west of the boundary. The important complex of petroglyphs at Puuloa is about 5 miles east of the boundary, probably too far to have any relationship to it. In Puna, at the boundary of the *ahupua'a* of Laeapuki and Kamoamoa, a dome-shaped *pahoehoe* mound called Puumanawalea (hill that brings together with rejoicing) covered with petroglyphs, marks the line. This same boundary is marked farther inland with a small group of petroglyphs at a point where the mountain trail crosses it. All these sites except the last mentioned are near the coast on an "upper" coast trail.

The largest group of petroglyphs on Kauai (numbering about 170) are those on the beach at Keoneloa on the boundary between the *ahupua'a* of Weliweli and Paa. These were first reported by Farley (1898) in his article "The Pictured Ledge of Kauai." His interest in the history of the petroglyphs led him to make many inquiries of natives in the area. Some of these accounts were passed on to John Stokes, who entered the following in some manuscript notes about the Keoneloa petroglyphs:

As further evidence of age of these petroglyphs I may briefly recount what Mr. Farley told me of an oral tradition. In a boundary dispute between the chiefs of the neighboring lands of Weliweli

Fig. 37. *Piko* holes, top of mound
Puuloa, Hawaii, HV-225

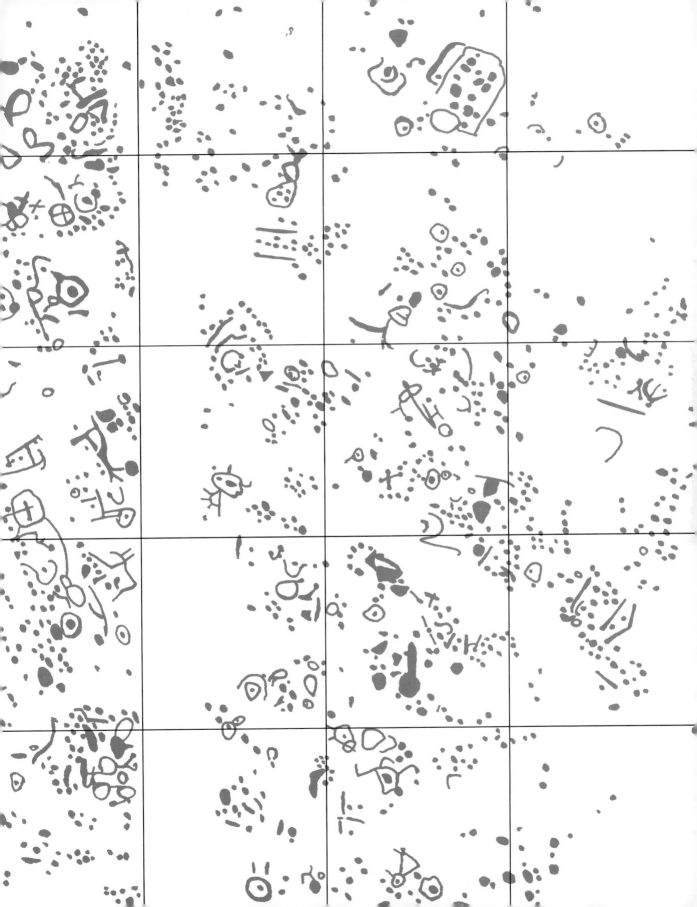

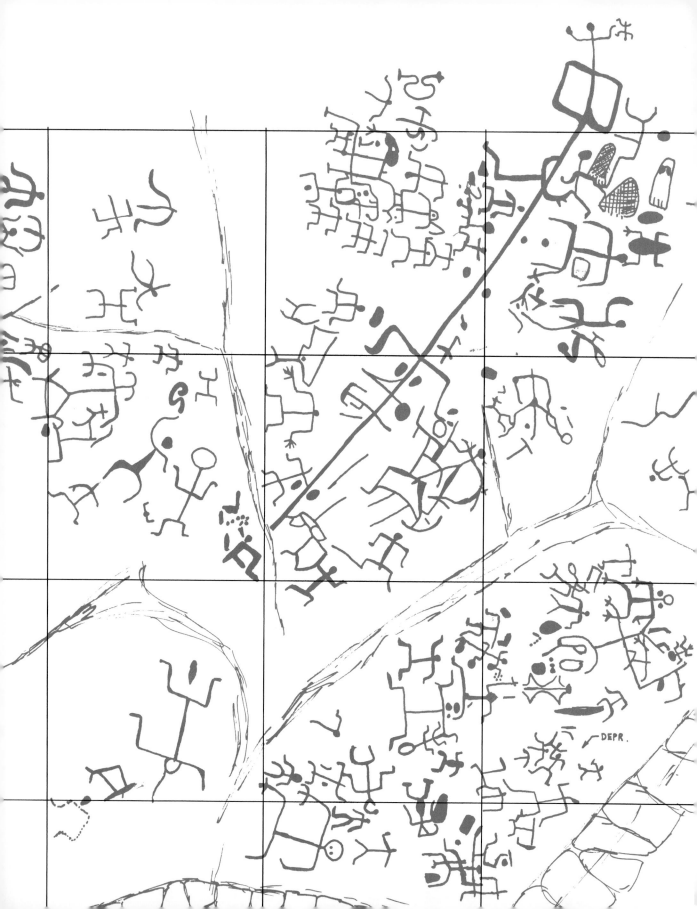

DEPR.

on the south and Paa on the north, it was agreed to settle the matter by the ancient style of arbitration—an appeal to arms. The terms were that the defeat of the Paa men would settle the boundary about the middle of the beach, and a victory of the same would place the boundary at the south end of the beach where the *ki'i* pictures were. The Weliweli men apparently lost the fight, and the boundary runs just south of the petroglyphs.

The larger "boundary" sites have dozens or even hundreds of petroglyphs, far more than would be needed for land division or trail marks. They, therefore, must have functioned in other ways as well. Under the *kapu* system, boundaries were inviolable, as noted above by Wise (1965). Trespass was a serious offense. Passage from one *ahupua'a* to another was not taken lightly, and the crossing of a district boundary was an even more rare and auspicious event. To pose a possibility and a question: some ritualistic act may have been needed to clear a *kapu,* to ask permission from the gods, or to insure the protection of one's *'aumakua* in the foreign land. Could the petroglyphs be an aspect of such an event? Considering this possibility and keeping in mind that there were probably a number of functions for petroglyphs, Ellis' statement about those he observed in Hawaii in 1824 could take on a rather different meaning than has previously been given to it.

Along the southern coast, both on the east and west sides, we frequently saw a number of straight lines, semicircles, or concentric rings, with some rude imitations of the human figure, cut or carved in the compact rocks of lava. They did not appear to have been cut with an iron instrument, but with a stone hatchet, or a stone less frangible than the rock on which they were portrayed. On inquiry, we found that they had been made by former travellers, from a motive similar to that which induces a person to carve his initials on a stone or tree, or a traveller to record his name in an album, to inform his successors that he had been there.

When there were a number of concentric circles with a dot or mark in the centre, the dot signified a man, and the number of rings denoted the number in the party who had circumambulated the island. When there was a ring and a number of marks, it denoted the same; the number of marks showing of how many the party consisted; and the ring, that they had travelled completely around the island; but when there was only a

Fig. 38.   Central area, Kaeo trail
Puako, Hawaii, E3-1

semicircle, it denoted that they had returned after reaching the place where it was made.

In some of the islands we have seen the outline of a fish portrayed in the same manner, to denote that one of that specie or size had been taken near the spot; sometimes the dimensions of an exceedingly large fruit, etc., are marked in the same way. (Ellis, 1917, p. 346.)

However, the motives for making the petroglyphs were likely to have been more urgent than Ellis suggests, probably founded in deeply felt needs: among them, satisfying the ego by leaving one's mark; identifying oneself with the group and recording this event; and insuring one's body and spirit against the consequences of not applying the available magic. Self-preservation, or at least personal well-being, was to be insured by the action taken. Although Ellis' report seems quite final and complete, it is unfortunate that it was not more detailed and consistent since it is the only first-hand account recorded during the period when petroglyphs were being made. It has been extremely valuable in establishing the purpose and meaning of some of the petroglyph forms, and has pointed the way for further investigation. Even though we may have no reason to question Ellis' accuracy in reporting, it is hardly reasonable to rest the entire case of the meanings of the petroglyphs on this one statement. The specific symbols that he described, dots and circles, apparently functioned in an alternate way at the Puna site of Puuloa. (If Ellis' inquiry was made at the Puuloa site itself, which has been suggested, then his informant was apparently not aware of the possibility of other meanings for the same marks.) Ellis' mention of the portrayal of fish and fruit also raises an interesting question. Where are these petroglyphs of fish and fruit? In all of the islands only two or three distinguishable pictures of fish are known, and there are no recognizable petroglyphs of fruit. One must conclude that this paragraph does not refer to the Hawaiian petroglyphs.

Reading carefully the two sentences that describe the meaning of the circles and dots, one finds that Ellis says that two different symbols, circles and dots, stand for the same thing: a person in a party of travelers; and that one symbol, the circle, stands for two things: trips and men. This seems like a contradiction of the idea that they are communicable symbols. In the case of the semicircles it is assumed that these are accompanied by dots to indicate the number in the party. Actually this is a rare combination. Semicircles are almost invariably found alone. In spite of these and other questions that might be asked about the exact meanings in the account, it does, however, establish that at the time the inquiry was made some of the dot and circle forms were intended as records of trips and a tally of individuals, but the specific details in this case are obscure.

This report by Ellis has been widely used by subsequent writers. Jarves (1843) and Lyman in 1846 (1924) give essentially the same interpretation. Jarves gives credit to Ellis for the information and there is no doubt that Lyman also used it because his wording is almost the same. In more recent times, with the renewal of interest in the petroglyphs, the Ellis account was often quoted as explaining the meanings of the petroglyphs. No doubt it does explain a function of some of them, but which ones is still a conjecture, and the complete meaning of circles and semicircles has not been made clear. The commemorative signature is only one of several uses to which the petroglyphs were put.

The activities at the boundaries at tax-collecting time, and the makahiki festival which followed, are other indications of the significance of the ahupua'a and district boundaries. There is no conclusive evidence that the petroglyphs that occur at some of these points played a part in the festival activities, but there is a distinct possibility that they did in some areas. At the time of tax-collecting and at the makahiki games, the procession of the Lono god image made use of the upper coastal trail. From Malo's description (1951, pp. 143-147) of the makahiki events, written about 1835, we can get a partial picture of these proceedings:

22.   This Makahiki idol was a stick of wood having a circumference of about ten inches and a length of about two

athoms. In form, it was straight and staff-like, with joints carved
t intervals and resembling a horse's leg; and it had a figure
arved at its upper end.

23.   A cross piece was tied to the neck of this figure and to
his cross piece, *kea*, were bound pieces of the edible *pala* fern.
rom each end of this cross piece were hung feather *lei* that
uttered about, also feather imitations of the *kaupu* bird, from
vhich all the flesh and solid parts had been removed.

26.   There was also an *akua poko* (short god); so called
ecause it was carried only as far as the boundary of the district
nd then taken back; also an *akua paani* (god of sports), which
ccompanied the *akua loa* (long god) on its tour of the island
nd was set up to preside at the assemblies for boxing, wrestling,
nd other games. By evening of the same day (Olepau), the
naking of the *akua loa* was complete.

30.   By the time the Makahiki god had arrived, the *konohiki*
et over the different districts and divisions of the land—known
s *kalana, okana, poko,* and *ahupuaa*—had collected the taxes
or the Makahiki, and had presented them as offerings to the god;
nd so it was done all round the island.

33.   As the idol approached the altar that marked the boundary
of the *ahupuaa* a man went ahead bearing two poles, or guidons,
alled *alia*.

37.   By this ceremony the land under consideration was sealed
s free. The idol was then turned face downwards and moved on
o signify that no one would be troubled, even though he ventured
n the left-hand side of the road, because the whole district had
een declared free from tabu, *noa*. But when the idol came to the
order of the next *ahupuaa*, the tabu of the god was resumed;
nd any person who then went on the left-hand side of it,
ubjected himself to the penalties of the law. Only when the
uardians of the idols declared the land free did it become free.

38.   This was the way they continued to do all round the
sland; and when the image was being carried forward its face
ooked back, not to the front.

This brief selection from Malo's description of the
makahiki is sufficient to indicate a number of important
lements: the emphasis on *kapu*, the strict compliance
vith ritual patterns, the use of symbols such as staffs
vith various attachments, and the importance of the
ahupua'a and district boundaries. In this and most other
descriptions of the *makahiki* it is stated that the procession
continued around the entire island. But it should be noted
hat certain activities must have stopped at district
oundaries. Certainly if the districts were under separate

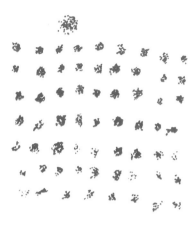

Fig. 39.   *Papamu*
Kealakomo, Hawaii, HV-335–(364)

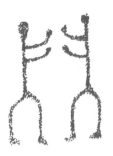

Fig. 40.   Boxers
Kalailinui, Maui, B22-2

and autonomous chiefs the taxes would not be shared across such boundaries. This aspect of the *makahiki* stopped at the district boundaries or at whatever point the chiefs' control terminated.

The *makahiki* is the only clearly described and authenticated ceremonial activity that is closely related to the land, products, boundaries, trails, and the assembling of large groups of people. In one way or another some of these elements are common to the petroglyphs. As an example, could the *makahiki* games between the districts of Kau and Puna have been held at the village of Kealakomo in South Puna? The area is well suited for it, open, fairly flat and at the union of trails from North Puna, Kau, and the mountain areas of Kilauea and Olaa. In the small area of the village site interspersed among numerous other petroglyphs there are 67 *papamu*, or rectangular areas marked in the *pahoehoe* with grids of small holes, for the game of *konane*. This number of game areas meets the needs of tournaments rather than occasional games between village residents. *Konane* tournaments may have been a minor feature of the *makahiki* games.

It has also been suggested that some of the petroglyphs in the Makawao district of Maui were made by a *makahiki*

party resting on an overland trip to the games. There are depicted here a number of pairs of boxers facing each other with arms in fighting position, and a number of canoes decorated with streamers which suggest the manner of their arrival, possibly from another island.

The unique group at the Puako site, a long line of 29 marching figures, flanked on either side by greatly extended figures about 6 feet long brings to mind a picture of the *makahiki* procession moving along a trail accompanied by the priests of Lono (Fig. 61). Not far from this group is another petroglyph which might first be taken as an unfinished human figure without legs but it could well be a picture of the Lono image, an upright staff with the head at the apex and a cross bar with banners suspended from it. Bennett in his sketches of the petroglyphs of Kauai (1931, Fig. 17) shows three figures (l, m, s) that are very like the Lono image and mentions that one of them "possibly [represents] an image on a pole."

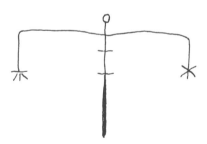

Fig. 41. Lono symbols
Puako, Hawaii, E3-1 (Paniau)

The above speculations relating petroglyphs to the *makahiki* activities are based on conjectural reasoning, but at least one Hawaiian account ties petroglyphs directly to tax collecting. The field notes of Martha Beckwith, an anthropologist who visited the Puuloa petroglyph site in Puna in 1915, relate that her guide, Konanui, explained the meaning of the markings there. Each of those on the top of the *pahoehoe* mound, mostly dots and circles, was made for the birth of a child, but other designs and figures which are on the flat areas around the mound, were "made by men who went around the district at the time of tax collecting and camped at this sacred spot." By his actions, Miss Beckwith suspected that the guide did not regard these latter figures to be as sacred as he did the dots and circles that cover the top of the mound. Although the *makahiki* procession is not named specifically in this record, the guide must have been referring to it as practiced during the prehistoric period, or at least premissionary times, because the system of collecting taxes by traveling parties was not carried on after 1821.

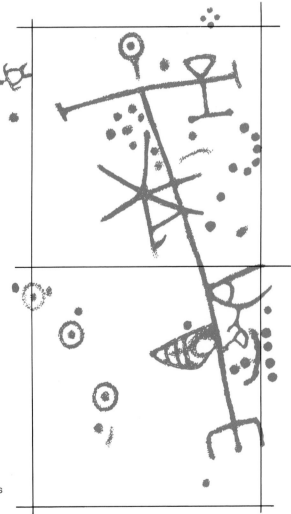

Fig. 42. Lono figure with sails
Puuloa, Hawaii, HV-225

Techniques

Hawaiian stone images *(ki'i pohaku)* are disappointing as works of art. Probably this was due to the preference by good craftsmen for wood and featherwork as worthy symbols for their gods. However, stone was used a good deal to represent family or craft gods *('aumakua)*. Some individuals were content to use pieces of unworked stone, whereas others made rough representations of the human figure. It should be remembered that it was not the workmanship but the prayers and offerings which gave a material object power *(mana)* and converted it into a god, no matter what the form. Thus any individual could make a stone god for himself; and the manufacture of gods, particularly by fishermen, continued for some time after the acceptance of Christianity. (Buck, 1957, p. 495.)

If the above is accurate, it might follow that, since many petroglyphs are certainly "rough representations of the human figure," Buck's opinion would be just as applicable to those many petroglyphs executed in the shape of a man.

On first view, the technical quality and craftsmanship evident in the Hawaiian petroglyphs do not compare favorably with those of the other arts, such as wood sculpture, tapa design, or featherwork. To some this may suggest that the petroglyphs were done by amateurs, that no craft was developed, or that they were insignificant in the culture. Actually a wide range of proficiency is evident even though the motifs and general configurations are limited. Before passing judgment on this level, consider that such a judgment is being made from a much larger sampling than exists in the other arts. Most of the petroglyphs ever made are probably still in existence. Not so with images, bowls, capes, or other movable objects, the poorer examples of which are discarded as unsuitable, worn out, or otherwise lost to posterity. Since all the petroglyphs survive, some will surely seem crude and formless, but many are carefully delineated and surprisingly sophisticated. All were purposefully made and most of them held an intense, though possibly temporary, significance for the maker.

Some differences in form and style as well as in craftsmanship are evident from site to site. These differences are caused, to a great extent, by the manner in

Fig. 44. Female figure Puako, Hawaii, E3-1

Fig. 43. An example of the bruising technique on boulders at Kukui Point, Lanai (LA-209). These ghost-like images are difficult to see since the weathering of the surface tends to obliterate the tone and texture differences. Note the joining of the upper figures and the faint marks to the left, which may also be more joined figures.

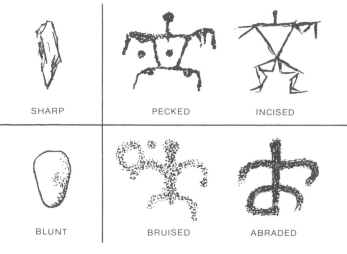

| SHARP | PECKED | INCISED |
| BLUNT | BRUISED | ABRADED |

Fig. 45. Tools and techniques

which they are made, which in turn is determined by three technical factors: (1) the character of the rock surface (which is described elsewhere); (2) the kind of tool used; and (3) the manner of applying the tool to the surface. A simple chart is given here to establish a useful terminology and to indicate in a general way the styles resulting from the kind of tool and the manner of its use.

Petroglyphs made after the 1800's could very well have been made with iron tools. The sharp-edged delineation of some of the lettering, dates, ships, and guns indicates the use of iron, but examples of this are not abundant. Stone was the common material for cutting, hammering, and rubbing. For the petroglyphs the working end of the stone tool was either blunt or sharply pointed, or less frequently knife-edged. It is puzzling that with thousands of petroglyphs at many sites on all the Hawaiian Islands so few appropriate implements are found for making them. A few instances are recorded of such tools being found at the petroglyph sites but there are no authenticated specimens in existence. Any heavy stone of sufficient hardness, or perhaps the common Hawaiian hammerstone, could have been used for a blunt pounder. A sharp chunk of compact basalt or a broken chisel or adz would make a useful sharp-pointed petroglyph tool. The tools were simple and unspecialized but effective. For pounding, the tool would need to be fairly heavy unless it was held against the surface and hit with a hammerstone. This chiseling technique (the use of a secondary tool) was used in wood carving and in the rough shaping of stone implements,* so it was in common enough use to have been adapted to petroglyph carving. There are occasional sites where no basalt of a compactness any harder than that of the surface *pahoehoe* is to be found. At the Kamooalii petroglyphs a thorough search was made of the surrounding area and the only foreign material found was a waterworn stone from the beach. It is likely here, at least, that an implement was brought to

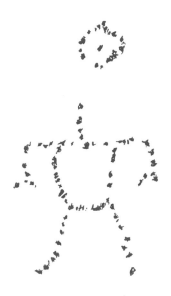

Fig. 46. Unfinished figure
Puuloa, Hawaii, HV-225

*According to K. P. Emory, from examination of the debris at the adz quarries on Mauna Kea.

e site, to be used and taken away again, or hidden. The implication is that one would set out purposefully to make petroglyph at Kamooalii, unless it can be assumed that was common practice for travelers to carry such tools.

For applying energy to the rock surface only two actions re possible: pounding or rubbing. With the blunt tool a ounding action bruised the surface causing the outer yer to break away exposing the color of the under layer. e possibility of controlling the edges of the shapes is nited and petroglyphs made by this method are simple, distinct, and soft-edged. An alternate method of oducing this type was by a rubbing action with the blunt ol or a combination of pounding and rubbing. The use of e blunt tool was not a very widespread practice. By far e greatest number of the petroglyphs were made with a narp-pointed stone. In general only one type was used at single site, one of the few exceptions being the island of anai, where suitable rock, usually boulders, would accept oth techniques.

A number of unfinished petroglyphs indicate the usual rocess of developing an image. With the sharp tool a line drawing was probably first scratched on the rock surface and adjustments made in scale, shape, and direction. Next, small holes would be pecked along the sketch lines about half an inch apart. The area between the holes was then broken away, forming a line with a fair regularity of width and depth. A drawing can be made rather quickly with this method, in perhaps half an hour for a small figure, but not fast enough to allow, or lead to, scribbling or random doodling. The technique demands a rather clear preconception of the desired image, followed by a fairly well-planned series of purposeful actions. Such a process is one of the factors that has led to a standardization of the forms of the petroglyphs to a simple lineal diagram and finally to those limiting characteristics which determine style.

The sharp tool, either pointed or knife-edged, was occasionally used with a rubbing action, producing the sharp-lined incised type of image (Fig. 8). The lines are usually straight and crisp, tending to overlap at the joints, the total reading more as an assembly of straight units than as one continuous configuration. This style was not

Fig. 47. A human figure of the basic lineal type. This shows the grooving formed by pecking. The penis and the hand on the left turning in toward the body have not been completed. (Site HA-B23-40)

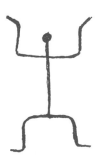

Fig. 48. Figure Puako, Hawaii, E3-1

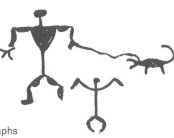

Fig. 49. Pictographs Waikonu, Maui, A16-1

Fig. 50.   Engraved figure
Puako, Hawaii, E3-1 (Kaeo trail)

Fig. 51.   Dancer with gourd
Puuloa, Hawaii, HV-225

Fig. 52.   Unfinished figures
Puuloa, Hawaii, HV-225

widely used and is found almost exclusively on boulder surfaces. Rubbing was also used to grind down the edges of some of the pecked figures (Fig. 58). This combination of pecking and rubbing produced some of the "best" petroglyphs; that is, those in which the lines are clear and regular in width, depth, and direction. It is in this formalized style that purposeful action is evident and the artist's intentions and his concern for form can best be appreciated.

The Hawaiian petroglyph technique depends entirely on texture and tone differences and the light and shadow of the cavities for the contrasts that make them visible. There is no evidence that color or black or white pigments were used in combination with the carvings. There are, however, a few painted pictures, properly called pictographs rather than petroglyphs. These are in the Hana district on the island of Maui. In general they are similar in form to the typical carved petroglyphs of the area, but the human figures tend toward a greater elongation of the torso and, because they are painted, have slightly more freedom of line than the petroglyphs exhibit. They are painted in a red pigment, probably a red-earth, on the lighter surfaces of vertical cliffs which have offered them some protection.

Since they are technically not petroglyphs they will not be discussed further here, except to note that these pictographs seem to be a localized variation of the usual petroglyph style of a fairly advanced and late type. There is nothing to suggest that their meaning or function would be different from the petroglyphs of the area.

An artist or artisan cannot be more technically proficient than his tools will allow. The tools limit the range of imagery and shape, and have a strong influence on design and expression.

Figure 50 is a very clear example of how the working tool has limited the range of imagery and shape and how the character and design of a simple image can have an effect on what that image seems to say to the observer. This petroglyph was executed by rubbing back and forth with a sharp-edged instrument, resulting in the extremely straight, dignified, somewhat elegant man-image. In Figure 51 the petroglyph was executed by pecking and, with the greater freedom of this method, a figure has been constructed which suggests strength, a more naturalistic concept of the man-image, and is powerful instead of elegant.

Fig. 56.   Unfinished circle
Puuloa, Hawaii, HV-225

Fig. 53.   Figure
Kukui Point, Lanai, 209

Fig. 54.   Figure with *piko*
Pohue Bay, Hawaii, B23-40

Fig. 55.   Circle and unfinished symbol
Kamooalii, Hawaii, HV-210.

It is also interesting to consider at this point the restraint used in Hawaiian petroglyphs in view of the potential for elaboration of designs into decorative surfaces realized in petroglyphs elsewhere, for example, in New Caledonia. The Hawaiians were capable of and enjoyed making surface decorations; the tapas and tattoos show this to be true. Apparently it was not important or relevant to the image to embellish it with the characteristic multiplicity of fine geometric patterns. The lava or boulder was not a support for decorations and the petroglyph was, so to speak, self-sufficient.

It is difficult to say whether it was always customary to make a preliminary design for a petroglyph. Certainly in the case of some of the more elaborate designs there would have had to be a very clear concept of what shapes were to be made. An image has to be adapted to its site, if not compositionally, then at least with a sense of scale and consideration for its size. There are so many simple figures that this particular shape would require little forethought except for some care in fitting it into a given space. However, there are some examples where such considerations were ignored and we find incomplete images as in Figure 52. In both cases, if the figures had

been completed in relative proportion they would have run into deteriorated surface material. It is possible that the surface deterioration came after the images were made, but that would seem to be too coincidental since none of the completed lines or shapes intrude into the poorly surfaced zone. There are many cases where figures and other images do cross into or through unsuitable surface material. This shows that the Hawaiians were simply inconsistent in their concern for surfaces. An example from Kukui Point on Lanai shows an imaginative use of a natural elipse from which a spear-carrying figure was constructed with the elipse used as the head. There is a similar occurrence at Pohue Bay, where a natural bubble on the surface is used as a *piko*.

In the case of simple imagery, for example, Figure 55 (from Kamooalii) shows a complete circle, with two others incomplete, which were in the process of being pecked out in a rather hit-and-miss manner. It is possible that a light line was scratched into the surface; but judging from the lack of concern for perfection here, it is unlikely any preparation was made. Figure 56 from Puuloa suggests that the circle was dotted in and then nearly completed before being abandoned.

Fig. 58.   These simple lineal angular figures are near the center of the Puako site (HA-E3-1). Two of the figures (left and upper left) seem unfinished, but these torso-like forms are numerous enough here and at other sites to suggest a special symbolism, possibly as bird forms. The large figure appears to have been reworked, possibly by rubbing. The small figure under the legs of the larger one is typical of the "family" or "birth" subjects at this site. The footprint is one of the few examples of overlapping in which the sequence is clearly evident.

Composition

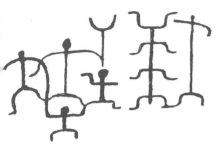

Fig. 57. Figure grouping
Puako, Hawaii, E3-1 (Kaeo trail)

In spite of the obvious fact that in some of the more concentrated sites the petroglyphs seem completely chaotic, and even in some less crowded areas the units might be described as a random scattering across the surface, a certain pattern and order does usually occur in their orientation with each other. This order is partly related to the characteristics of the units themselves— the petroglyph style. The human figures are schematic, lineal, usually frontal, and bisymmetric. Other forms are likewise oriented to their most descriptive position—dogs, chickens, and pigs are seen from the side, turtles from the top, birds from underneath. Although the elements of this style are extremely simple, they can be surprisingly expressive. The style can be manipulated into variations that allow for complex interpretations of forms, groupings, space relationships, and actions.

Certainly few petroglyphs that are in groups were intended as pictorial units. Some are independent figures having no apparent relationship with the others either in time or space. The first carver in a given area felt a certain physical, visual, and scale orientation to his format—the boulder face or *pahoehoe* slab—and proceeded accordingly. The second and later artists often oriented their work not only to their own needs but also to any already existing figures, since the space was thereby limited. This practice continued until the area was so filled that the artists were forced to ignore the previous images and carved new figures on top of old ones (Fig. 73). At Puako, overlapping of imagery indicates an apparent lack of concern for what happened to the earlier images. This is convincing evidence that in such areas the special importance of a particular space demanded that the images be placed there.

When groups of figures or elements do have an interrelationship or common meaning, that is, are composed, the system of structuring the units, as used by the Hawaiians, is similar to those used by primitive man in general. The Hawaiians did, however, invent some systems that are unique. It is likely that the figures were not thought of as illustrating the appearance of people,

Fig. 59. Composite figure
Kukui Point, Lanai, 209

Fig. 60. One end of a line of angular figures at Paniau
(HA-E3-1). This particular group has figures of two clearly
different sizes. Compare to Figure 61 from the same general area.

ut only as a symbol for them (or their spirits). Likewise
here was no thought of the surroundings of the figures as
pace in the physical sense. There is no gravity, no ground
ne, no ground surface, no background, consequently no
verlapping or foreshortening or perspective. Since size
ifferences in a group are apparently descriptive rather
han symbolic, that is, children are little and adults are
igger, they are all at the same distance, on a single plane.
cale change may indicate status or rank (as in the
narching line flanked by the large figures at Puako), but
his device was not in general practice. Figures are often
oined or several figures will have parts in common with
thers. This may completely obscure the individuals, but
o the artist it was probably a way of indicating the
articular relationship between them. A simple example of
his is in the long lines with multiple legs—centipede-like
igures—that are very probably a group of human figures
n single file. This becomes more understandable when
hey are compared to the long line of "marching men" at
Paniau, which can only be a line of men in single file on a
rail. Front views side by side would produce a static row
and the ground line suggested by the position of the feet
vould be contrary to the Hawaiian sense of space),
herefore a head-to-foot position is the logical method of
depicting the scene. Since all figures are frontal, the
owest figure in the line is facing the "viewer" and is
closest and the top one is farther away. This is contrary
o the Western orientation of most observers which places
he uppermost figure in the lead. Consequently the group
s advancing "downward." In the "centipede" forms the
igures are in close ranks, too close together to be seen
as individuals, the bodies merging into a single line. If this
concept of frontality and space relationship is correct, it
nay clarify some other figure groupings. For example, the
wo figures head to head at Kapalaoa would then be a
convention for figures standing back to back.

It is often difficult to know the intended meanings of the
relationships between various units of a composition, but
n some cases family groups seem to be indicated. In a
number of instances an open figure will have a smaller

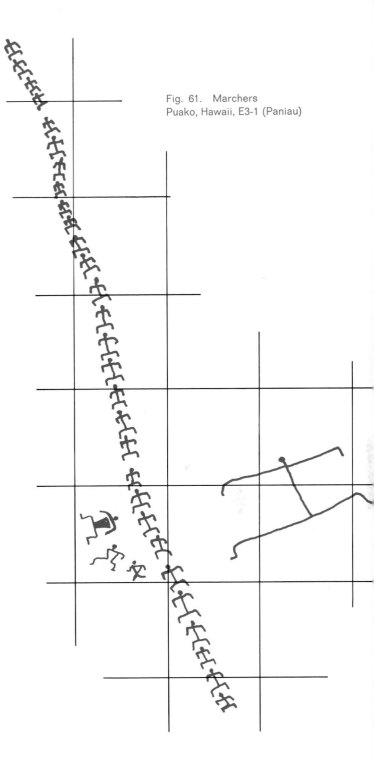

Fig. 61.   Marchers
Puako, Hawaii, E3-1 (Paniau)

Fig. 62. "Centipede" composite
Luahiwa, Lanai, 177

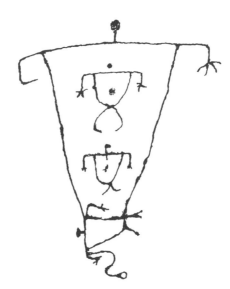

Fig. 64a. Pregnancy and birth
Pakininui, Hawaii, B22-12

Fig. 65. Figure grouping
Puako, Hawaii, E3-1 (Kaeo trail)

Fig. 63. Mirrored figures
Kapalaoa, Hawaii, D24-6

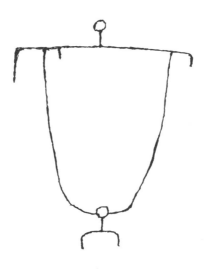

Fig. 64b. Birth scene
Puuloa, Hawaii, HV-225

Fig. 66. Family groups
Puako, Hawaii, E3-1 (Kaeo trail)

Fig. 67. The birth scene at Puako site (HA-E3-1) described on page 48. The two male figures, father and son, are of the triangular body, muscled type, in which the surface is pecked out as a shape in contrast to the female forms which are in schematic outline with open torsos.

Fig. 68. Birth scene
Puako, Hawaii, E3-1 (Kaeo trail)

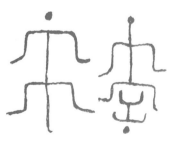

Fig. 69. Birth scene
Kahuluu, Hawaii, D4-4

47

figure within it, perhaps indicating a pregnant woman, or small figures will be attached to larger ones, suggesting children with parents. At the Kaeo site the great number of such probable family groups has led to the suggestion that this area may have some special meaning in this regard, possibly a parallel to the holes and circles which feature in the birth rites at Puuloa, Puna, on the opposite side of the island.

On the northern edge of the Kaeo site a particularly descriptive family group must certainly narrate the story of the birth of an *ali'i* child (Fig. 67). The father and mother are side by side. The figures are larger than the average petroglyphs, about 3 feet high and somewhat more elaborate, which probably indicates their importance. The male's body is a wide triangle, the surface of which is entirely pecked out. The female's body is equally wide but rounded rather than angular, the vulva is shown as a large circular cavity, much deeper than any other marks in the area. On her shoulder is a girl child, judging by the open torso. The father is holding another child by the feet with its head down. The head of this child is of particular importance. It is stylized as a horizontal bar with vertical comb-like bars rising from it, perhaps the crest symbol of a high chief.

Stokes (1910, pp. 262–263) describes a similar scene in the pictures at Kahaluu, Kona:

The pictures of the interesting quartet in the foreground of Fig. 7 are no doubt an attempt to portray the happenings at an obstetrical case; the figures are grouped together and are slightly removed from the rest of the pictures. Kahaluu, from its superior natural advantages, was the abode of many chiefs and kings (as the number of heiau in the vicinity would indicate), and this group may well have been intended to record the not uncommon occurrences in Hawaiian history such as mentioned by Fornander [1880] in vol. ii, pp. 204 and 260.

The petroglyphs Stokes refers to here are a group of three simple lineal figures, a large male figure, a smaller female figure with a still smaller one, the child, head down between the legs of the female.

Fig. 70. The complex overlapping of units at Anaehoomalu (HA-E1-1); detailed analysis on opposite page.

As has already been suggested, some of the highly complex arrangements of images are probably the result of a succession of artists working in a limited area. In some it may be possible through careful observation to suggest the sequence of such events. If a number of such analyses could be made, some clues to relative dating of the petroglyphs might result. Such examination can also suggest some of the decisions and habits of the artists.

Some years ago Kenneth Emory and a party from Bishop Museum carefully examined a complex of markings next to the heavily worn horse trail at the Anaehoomalu site (Fig. 70). The result is shown in Figure 71a-d which illustrates a possible sequence of drawings on the slab. It also destroyed some fanciful imaginings about the meaning of the elaborate complex, which, taken in its finished state, suggested to some that this was how the Hawaiians must have pictured some mysterious demon spirit.

The first unit placed on the irregular elongated area was a simple, lineal, angular figure of the widely accepted style. It is rather large, about 4 feet long, and was placed vertically to fit the existing space, and to dominate the empty format. It was carefully made, with uniform lines, showing a better technical control than the marks which followed. The rectangular head was apparently a planned part of this figure—not a later elaboration. The small figure to the lower right may also have been an early addition to the space. It is compositionally aligned and in a considered relationship to the large figure. Other shapes followed, first probably the shapes near the head, the partial figure to the left of the smaller one and the circles with dots. The arch over the head, possibly a rainbow symbol such as those found in other petroglyphs, was applied after the circle and rod to the right of the head was in place. This symbol, which is normally a regular parabola, was necessarily altered in this case to avoid the existing marks. The fingers and the feet, for which new legs were added, were probably on an unmarked surface when they were drawn, but at a later time parts of them were obliterated or added to. Possibly one of the last

Fig. 71a-d. Figure complex
Anaehoomalu, Hawaii, E1-1

49

Fig. 72. Female figure
Puako, Hawaii, E3-1

Fig. 73a–d. On this hillside boulder at the Luahiwa site on Lanai (LA-177), an attempt was made to indicate the time sequence of the petroglyphs by the observation of overlapping, style-subject, and erosion. The most recent figures are shown in "a". Most of them are deeply cut and are superimposed on other figures, in some cases obliterating them. They show little erosion. Some of the subject matter proves them to be post-contact, such as the gun held by the figure at the lower right. The depiction of men on horses cannot be older than about 1800. (Horses were first introduced in 1798.) In low center there is what appears to be a man on a surfboard. The second level, "b", shows some erosion and in some cases figures are overlapped by those in "a". A horse is cut by a dog leash, held by the figure in the upper center. The other "animals" appear to be dogs. Most of the figures are filled in, rather than outlined. The figures of "c" and "d" are more obscure and the differences between the two levels are extremely difficult to detect. Overlapping is clear only in one or two places. What might be a horse and rider occurs in "c". The figures are generally more linear but even in "d" triangular figures occur, one of which is filled in. On the entire boulder, there appear to be no simple single-line human figures. Since the extent of erosion can only be estimated, decisions based on this factor cannot be very accurate. In some cases the sequence of overlapped elements cannot be determined. More studies of this nature would need to be made before a historic sequence of petroglyphs could be codified. Based on evidence from other studies, it would appear that most of the petroglyphs on this boulder are not very old, although some are probably from the pre-contact period.

elaborations was the line on the right of the torso that was carefully drawn to avoid touching the already existing foot and the other designs in its path. The dots and bars on the torso are so closely related to the vertical lines that it seems they must have been made after those lines were in place. Each successive artist had proceeded with a respect for existing work, maintaining a sense of clarity by controlling the size, position, and direction of his images. Intersections of lines are at right angles, which does the least damage to the clarity of each line.

It is not possible to know the purpose of this compulsion to add to and change an existing image. The forms appear to be deliberate, patterns were apparently planned, although they may have aspects of randomness. The activity seems purposeful rather than casual, with meaningful rather than merely decorative intent.

Although it may not be sound practice to extrapolate too freely from the analysis of only one such complex assembly, a number of possibilities suggest themselves; for example, that lineal figures are earlier than other forms; that circles are intermediate in this sequence; that workmanship deteriorated with time; that each mark had an independent meaning; and that a number of other inferences having to do with the aesthetic judgments of the artists could also be made.

Most of the conclusions and speculations about the Hawaiian petroglyphs are developed from those found on the island of Hawaii. It is there that the largest numbers, the most dense concentrations, and the greatest variety of forms and styles are found. In terms of numbers, the island of Hawaii probably has more petroglyphs than any other area of equal size in the world. It is also significant that this is the only area in the world from which there is fairly direct documented information about petroglyphs, given by informants who were living during the time they were still being made. On Hawaii are found what seem to be the newest, and also some of the oldest Polynesian petroglyphs, indicating a continuing practice that apparently died out in the other islands of Polynesia.

Age

If we rule out the possibility that the petroglyphs were made by some people other than the Hawaiians, there seem to be only three possible choices as to the time and nature of their origin: (1) The practice of making petroglyphs was brought by the first arrivals and continued for the entire history of the people; (2) The practice was introduced by later Polynesian arrivals; (3) The making of petroglyphs was an independent invention of the Hawaiians.

The first possibility would give the petroglyphs an exceedingly long history, but this does not mean that the activity of making them was at an equal level for the entire period of 1,200 years or more. It is certainly possible that the first discoverers of the Hawaiian Islands could have been familiar with the technique. A few petroglyphs may have been made by the first settlers, following a tradition of their homeland, and the trait would have been emplanted in Hawaii. Then at some time, probably late in the prehistoric period, some stimuli caused a rapid expansion of the art, resulting in the heavily concentrated sites that we know today. This sequence of events would also account for the number of forms that are peculiar to Hawaii and not found in other Polynesian areas, since elaboration and invention of new forms is a natural result of continued or intensive activity in the arts.

If the making of petroglyphs was introduced by later arrivals, one would expect more similarity between the Hawaiian types and those of the Society Islands or the Marquesas Islands. There are some basic similarities in the petroglyphs from these areas and those in Hawaii, but they are not sufficient to indicate a strong or recent influence. The slight similarities between all Polynesian areas in their sculpture and other arts is well known, indicating a common origin in the distant past. However, the differences in style among the areas indicate long periods of isolation, causing distinct style developments in each area.

An independent invention of petroglyph making in Hawaii is most unlikely, although not entirely impossible. For those reasons mentioned above, an early introduction

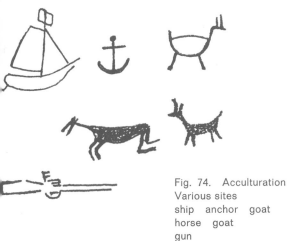

Fig. 74. Acculturation
Various sites
ship   anchor   goat
horse   goat
gun

One other factor that points to the period just prior to European discovery as an active one for the making of petroglyphs is that there was enough impetus in the making of them for a shift in subject—to sailing ships and guns—to occur as soon as these impressive objects were on the scene. These pictures would not have been made if the pattern had not already been set by a habit of making petroglyphs. Goats and horses, both introduced in about 1800, are depicted within the old style, with simplicity and a great deal of charm. They are so clearly characterized in action and spirit that they leave no doubt as to the penetrating insight of the artists and a ready familiarity with the practice of making petroglyphs. There are many names, enigmatic lettering, and some dates, even in some of the old sites. These are carefully constructed, generally in Roman capital letters, but script is found in a few places. It is curious that there are few dates earlier than 1860, and that most of the dates fall within this decade,* even though writing was introduced as early as 1821 and instruction in reading and the printing of books soon followed. This education, of course, began on a very limited scale, but even by 1831, 52,000 pupils were in school, and over half of the adult population was able to read (Kuykendall, 1938, p. 108). There has been a reasonable assumption that the names and dates, which are often connected to, or in association with, circles and dots or human figures, are extensions of the practice mentioned by Ellis of leaving a record of a trip through the district. In view of the idea of the birth custom at Puuloa accompanied by the making of dots and circles, it might also be conjectured that the lettering and figures could relate to some similar ceremony, in which the name and date of birth were indicated rather than the date of the making of the petroglyph. However, until there is more evidence relating to these late petroglyphs, the former theory seems more reasonable.

*Dates later than the 1860's do not occur because this period marked the virtual end of the petroglyph activity. The small Hawaiian villages and isolated homesites were being abandoned and travel by the old foot and horse trails was being replaced by use of wheeled vehicles on improved roads.

of a simple form from the homeland of the Hawaiians seems the most reasonable assumption.

It has not been possible so far to establish more than relative age for the petroglyphs. There is sufficient evidence that they were being made in the period just prior to discovery. Emory (1924, p. 115) has pointed out that human figure and other designs closely similar to petroglyphs were used in tattooing recorded by visiting artists before 1820. Some of the more elaborate muscled and almost sculptured figures were certainly reflecting an influence from the images sculptured in wood, and this style in the image sculpture was not reached until near the period of discovery of the islands by Captain Cook in 1778. The Puuloa site was still being used as a place for the *piko* ceremony until the 1860's, though by then not at a very heavy rate. The amount of erosion of the marks on the center mound of this site, compared with the newer petroglyphs in the surrounding area, is proof of a long and continuous history for the site.

Fig. 75. Church
Anaehoomalu, Hawaii, E1-1

WAIAHOLE
1862

Fig. 76. Name, date
Anaehoomalu, Hawaii, E1-1

From the earliest arrival of the Hawaiians to the late 1800's, then, the petroglyphs were being chipped into the Hawaiian landscape. The extent of the activity certainly varied at different times and, as the above evidence indicates, was probably more concentrated toward the end of the prehistoric period and the beginning of the historic. The petroglyph material has so far not been keyed into archaeological dates and there seems to be little chance of so doing. Some specific dates might be supplied if lava flows or rock formation could be dated within reasonable limitations, or if it were possible to measure erosion of chipped *pahoehoe,* or to date water-level changes on beach shelves where petroglyphs are now under water. Although there has been research in geology in these general areas, the defined time scale is still too broad to have very significant meaning in relation to Hawaiian history. Some petroglyphs on beach shelves have been inundated since their making by the subsidence of the beach land. The Keoneloa site on Kauai is one of these. Farley (1898) noted this and states:

As the ledge on which the pictures are made is, when free of sand, only partly exposed at low tide, and then nearly covered with water by every good sized wave, a natural conclusion is that the beach has subsided at least six feet since the pictures were cut. . . . The upper half of the ledge was dark and well glazed over, and the gravings on it were worn to the same appearance.

Other shore sites, Kahaluu and Anaehoomalu beaches on Hawaii, and Keaau and Pupukea-Koolauloa on Oahu, are at times covered with sand and water at high tide, but changes as great as 6 feet are not indicated, as Farley observed for Keoneloa. According to Hawaiian tradition the figure at the water's edge at Kahaluu, Kona, Hawaii, which is under water at high tide, would have a date of about 1600. It is said to represent the headless body of Kamalalawalu who was killed in battle by Lonoikamakahik and sacrificed at the *heiau* of Keeku, which is nearby.

For the present, means of establishing relative age of the petroglyphs must rely upon evidence of super-imposition, differences in technique, subject matter, and style—determining when or in what sequence these differences occurred.

The brief discussion of the complex assembly at Anaehoomalu indicates possibilities in this direction. Emory (1924, pp. 94–103), in his account of the petroglyph at Kaunolu village and at Luahiwa, Lanai, demonstrates that distribution and style differences can be used to some extent to determine the relative age of the petroglyphs on Lanai, and the theory is applicable to other areas as well. It is based on the idea that there were favored areas for making the carvings, that these areas would be used first, and that therefore the petroglyphs in these centers would be older. Those petroglyphs farther from the center, or

Fig. 77. Lettering
Anaehoomalu, Hawaii, E1-1

uperimposed ones, would have been made at a later date.
mory also suggests that an even and wide distribution of
style is likely to indicate a basic and older form. On this
asis he concludes that on Lanai the simple linear style is
lder and that the triangular-bodied forms and other
ariations are later.

The same reasoning would seem to apply at the heavily
concentrated site of Kaeo at Puako in Hawaii. The
eremonial center was certainly that area of highly
omplex assemblies of simple linear figures, connected
nd interlocked (Fig. 58). At the outer areas, along the
Kaeo trail, triangular, columnar, and muscled figures are
ar more numerous than the simple lineal ones and other
ubjects and elaborations are evident, such as sails,
addles, animals, and lettering.

The distribution of the symbols at Puuloa, Puna, Hawaii,
ndicates a similar sequence of events, providing evidence
hat at this site the dot and circle are the oldest units,
ollowed by various abstract forms and human figures.
Across the top of the mound of *pahoehoe* are the oldest
units, dots, circles, and bars, marking the center of the
acred area, the most favored place for depositing the
umbilical cord of the new-born child. At the center of
highest concentration, which covers an area about 20 feet
wide by 150 feet long, these marks are crowded and
overlapped, and the oldest are considerably eroded

Fig. 78. Circles and figures
Pohue Bay, Hawaii, B23-40
Puuloa, Hawaii, HV-225
Kailua, Hawaii, D9-4
Puuloa, Hawaii, HV-225

Fig. 79. Name, date, symbols
Anaehoomalu, Hawaii, E1-1

(Fig. 32). There are approximately 7,000 units in this central area. When the central area was no longer usable, the ceremonial pits were made on the surrounding lower surfaces, but were then farther apart and interspersed with other designs—crosses, dots connected to long curving lines, elaborate abstract shapes, and a few human figures of the triangular style (Fig. 81). None of these show the heavy erosion or crowding that occurs on the crest of the mound, and hence are probably newer.

Dots and circles are found almost exclusively on the island of Hawaii and are widely distributed there. This fact and their obvious age at Puuloa suggest that these simple symbols are probably as old as the basic lineal human figure.

Puuloa is of particular significance because it is the only site for which a specific function has been recorded. Because it was still in use in the late 1800's, some of the older residents of Puna were able to relate some specific information about the meanings of the symbols found

there. In 1914 the anthropologist Beckwith (n.d.) recorded in her field notes the following:

Rode out to Puuloa on the line between Kealakomo and Apuki. Here is a large *pahoehoe* mound used as a depository for the umbilical cord *(piko)*, at the birth of a child. A hole is made in the hard crust, the cord is put in and a stone is placed over it. In the morning the cord has disappeared—there is no trace of it. This insures long life for the child.

Mrs. Kama, born 1862, was a native of Kamoamoa. Her mother brought her cord here. She had 15 children and for each one at birth the visit was made to Puuloa.

Another mound, on the southern [*sic*] boundary of Apuki called Puu Manawalea was similarly used. This mound meant the bringing of the people together with rejoicing. Both mounds have the marks remaining of these visits, Puuloa is especially rich. There are holes, pictures, initials chiseled into the rocks. . . .

A resident of Kalapana, David Konanui, was Beckwith's guide and informant on the horseback trip, some 20 miles down the deserted and barren coast to Puuloa. In 1959 one of the authors made the same trip with Sam Konanui, the son of Beckwith's guide. Konanui was then 72 but remembered well the stories related by his father. He told this one about Puuloa:

This is the story of the *piko* at Pu'uloa. When I was small, going with my papa to fish, my papa explained the meaning of the doings of Pu'uloa. Pu'uloa means long life, and that is why they chose Pu'uloa to deposit the *piko* of their children.

You make a *puka* (hole) by pounding with a stone, then in the *puka* you put the *piko,* then shove a stone in the place where the *piko* is placed. The reason for putting in that stone is to save the *piko* from the rats. My papa said that if a rat took the *piko,* that child would become a thief; that's why it was covered with a stone.

Another thing that my papa said was that people on all the islands did the same thing. When they had babies, they saved all the *pikos* in an *'umeke* (calabash). When they had no more babies they would get on a canoe and bring the *piko* to Pu'uloa. Because they liked the [connotation of the] name Pu'uloa, which means long life they would bring the *piko* here, from all the islands to Hawaii nei. If they had ten children they would make ten *pukas.* Each *puka* held one *piko* and a small stone was inserted in each. They made the holes round in a ring so they know they belonged to one family. (Emory, Cox, and others, 1959, pp. 56–59.)

In a more recent conversation with Sam Konanui (in [19]66) I asked him if his own *piko* was taken to Puuloa. [H]e said it was buried by his father at his own birthplace in [S]outh Puna and a peach tree was planted over it. He took [si]x of his own ten children's *piko* to Puuloa in a calabash [an]d pecked holes with a stone and put them in. (This [ev]ent must have been as late as the 1920's.) He could not [re]member exactly where he had made the holes but [kn]ew they were not on top of the mound but on the lower [fla]t area. He related again that the circles with many [ho]les (one has 62) were made by families from Oahu, [M]aui, and even Kauai, who brought the *piko* of their [ch]ildren here in calabashes because they had heard of [th]e *mana* of the place. There seemed to be in his remarks [an]d gestures the suggestion that the circles represented [th]e calabash in which the *piko* were carried—as well as [in]dicating the family group. In Beckwith's field sketches [of] various petroglyphs seen at Puuloa a circle is labeled [u]meke (calabash).

By 1868 all of the coastal villages south of Kalapana [in]cluding Kamoamoa, Leapuki, Kealakomo, Apua, and [Ke]auhou) were deserted, partly because of the disastrous [e]arthquakes and tidal waves of that year. Except for a [fe]w local families, this probably marked the end of the [u]se of the Puuloa site for the *piko* ceremony. The practice [ha]d probably been greatly diminished long before this by [m]issionary activity and increasing contact with Western [ci]vilization after 1820. So, at Puuloa as in all other sites, [th]e petroglyphs for the most part were made in the [pr]ehistoric period.

All of the evidence concerning the relative age of the [p]etroglyphs points to a style sequence in time starting [w]ith simple forms and ending with complex ones. Judging [fr]om the development in the other arts such as tapa [m]aking, sculpture, and featherwork, the Hawaiian artists [w]ere on an ever ascending development in perfection [o]f techniques, refinement, and elaboration of forms. [A]lthough the petroglyphs cannot be compared to these [a]rts in sophistication or in flexibility of style, they were [a]lso on an ascending and not a descending style

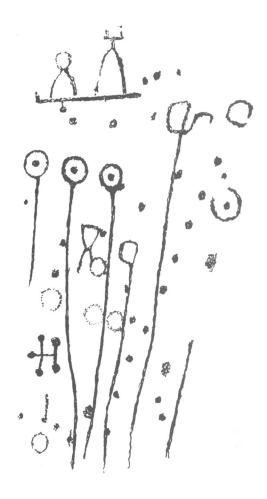

Fig. 80.   Circles with lines, figures
Puuloa, Hawaii, HV-225

Fig. 81. The lower sections of Puuloa have a greater variety of
symbols than the top of the mound (Fig. 32) but the dot groups
and circle motives still prevail.

development, starting with simple and occasionally crude symbols some time in the distant past, and were continually being adjusted to more complicated forms which would allow for extended and subtler meanings. In general, it seems that in the evolution of forms in art, images do not begin with naturalism and move toward abstraction unless other functions become more important than that of the image itself. Where the image is an end in itself the evolution will be from a simple form (possibly abstract as in the petroglyphs) to a more elaborate (and possibly naturalistic) form. However, images occurring on some object which has a function independent of the images (such as the decorations on the base of a Hawaiian drum) will be more apt to evolve from naturalistic to abstract.

There are hundreds of variations within the main types of petroglyphs, and some that do not fit, that are outside the main style trend. Some of these variations are due to individual differences in interpretation and skill. However, the over-all style maintains its general unity because only those variations and inventions that have meaning within the already established limits of communication are absorbed and become an aspect of style. Such random elements as scribbling, nonsense sounds, or accidental patterns are not influential in extending the means of established forms in writing, music, or the arts. New forms must be tied to the meaningful elements of the existing style and have relevance within the cultural context if they are to survive and flourish. The fact that the human figures, symbols, and cryptic marks have so much consistency, both over a wide area and over a considerable period of time, is the best proof that they can not be casual doodles or frivolous drawings.

The sequence of human images was probably thus: simple lineal angular figures; triangular and columnar outlined figures; the triangular outlined figure with angular muscles added; the filled in, curved muscular figure; and finally relief figures in which some modeling of the round surface is suggested; these are all incised below the surface of the rock (Fig. 83).

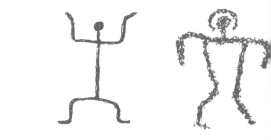

Fig. 82. An elaborately muscled figure, possibly a dancer with a gourd rattle. (See drawings of dancers by Choris and by Webber, pages 554 and 555 in Buck, 1957.)
The edges of the torso are deeply pecked and the chest is rounded as in a sculptured relief. These specialized features suggest that it is a late style in the petroglyph chronology. (Puuloa HV-225.)

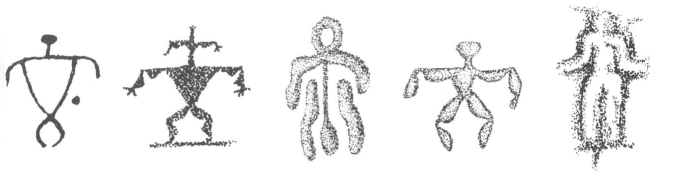

Fig. 83. Age sequence
Various sites

A similarity in general posture and attitude between the triangular, muscled, and modeled petroglyphs and the Hawaiian image sculpture in wood has already been mentioned. This marks the point of distinction between the Hawaiian petroglyphs and those of the rest of the world. If one were to ask—what aspect of the petroglyphs here is truly and exclusively Hawaiian?—the answer could be: the muscled figures. The next logical step in this apparent move toward naturalism and elaboration would be a true relief in which the surface of the surrounding rock is lowered, leaving the figure raised. There is one sample of this treatment (see Stokes, 1908, pp. 31-37), the Moanalua relief, a boulder now at Bishop Museum, but this is technically outside the limits of true petroglyphs. Accompanying this time sequence of human figures was a development of abstract symbols, probably starting with a single dot and circle and then combining these with other marks in increasingly more complicated forms. The simpler and earlier forms of both the human figures and abstractions, and all the subsequent inventions, continued to be used along with the newer ones. This accounts for the greater number and wider distribution of the basic types.

If it can be determined, as the above evidence indicates, that the earliest Hawaiian petroglyphs were the simple lineal figure and the dot and circle motif, it will most surely follow that the two oldest sites in the island must be those at Puako and Puuloa. The primary forms dominate in each of these sites—figures at Puako and dots and circles at Puuloa. Both fields are very extensive, the largest in the islands; and in the central areas of each the images are crowded and overlapped. At Puuloa, the central area—the top of the hill—is so heavily eroded as to almost obliterate the earliest of the carvings. In contrast to the heavy concentration at the center, the units thin out at the periphery of the site and are accompanied by more varied and complex forms which appear to be newer. It is of some interest to note that although the forms that were used at the two sites are different, the functions are similar. At both places, the petroglyphs seem to be protective symbols relating to birth, to children, and to families. The emphasis and concern placed on these things by the Hawaiians is well known. In this instance these needs seem to have supplied the incentive for the making of the very first petroglyphs in Hawaii.

Fig. 84.   Rectilinear forms are rare in the Hawaiian petroglyphs.
This square enclosure in association with a crude human figure is
at Kamooalii, Hawaii (HV-210).

Imagery and Symbolism

There are three subject categories in Hawaiian petroglyphs: the descriptive, the symbolic, and the cryptic.

The overwhelming number in which the subject is recognizable, the descriptive category, are found to deal with variations of the anthropomorphic image. Next in number are dots and circles, also with variations (Fig. 34). Almost all the others show a concern for a limited number of man-made objects and animals of importance to the Hawaiians. The number of recognizable subjects, then, is small. But there is a sizable amount of unclear markings (Fig. 92). These undeciphered symbols have led to much conjecture and to extreme theories with very little basis in fact; simply, there is almost no information for establishing meaning, or for an interpretation, of these petroglyphs.

Other than the man image and the unexplained group, there is an interesting pattern to the other subjects. There is a surprising lack of interest in natural forms and in nature itself. For example, in a land surrounded by the ocean, and which depended upon fish for a substantial part of its subsistence, there are practically no fish or marine life of any kind portrayed by the makers of petroglyphs. Other than a few turtles, crabs, and some other scarcely discernible sea creatures, sea life was largely neglected. There are no identifiable representations of fruits or vegetables, and only one spiral, a frequent symbol for growth and growing things. There are only a few petroglyphs which appear to represent chickens, and a few pigs, which were very important food items. To further confuse the matter, there are many images of dogs, which were important as pets as well as food. There are few, if any, flying birds; but, especially on Lanai, there are human figures with wing-like forms encroaching upon or attached to the upper torso and head (Fig. 22). Among man-made objects are representations of fishhooks, canoes, sails, and paddles, all of which are essential to kinds of fishing, but, of course, very few fish. Also notably absent from treatment are houses (unless some of the angular "enclosures" can be so construed), clothed figures (except one or two possibly

Fig. 85. Hawaiian artifacts
Various sites
fishhooks   poi pounder   canoe, paddles
paddle-man   man, adz, sail   sail
holua sled   spear man
man in cape   man on surfboard   cape
man with "staff"   *kapu* stick   fan   dancer with gourd

Fig. 86. Endemic animals
Various sites
turtle   chicken   dog
bird   crab   dog
birds(?)   bird   pig

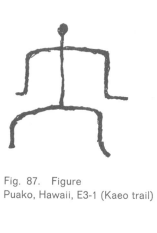

Fig. 87.   Figure
Puako, Hawaii, E3-1 (Kaeo trail)

Fig. 88.   Gesturing figure
Kamooalii, Hawaii, HV-210

caped figures), references to rain or water of any kind, fire, volcanic activity, trees, flowers, or geographical features. Among postdiscovery period subjects there are some rifles, square-rigged sailing ships, a church with a spire, lettering (in almost all cases names and dates), goats and horses (Figs. 74, 75, 76).

There is no consistent presentation of imagery in Hawaiian petroglyphs. For example, a dog may be represented with one ear or two, two legs or four; but the human figure is almost exclusively depicted from a frontal view showing two arms, two legs, and most often, no fingers. When fingers are attached to the arm they are most often three in number. In general, excellent judgment is used in choosing the most characteristic view of the subject depicted. When a petroglyph is descriptive of something it is usually readily identifiable. This ability of the carver to single out pictorially significant detail and to be able to simplify and still clearly express the nature and physical appearance of things suggests an intention to be clear and specific. This makes it even more difficult to unravel the meanings of the huge number of cryptic carvings. It is most often easy to establish that a petroglyph represents a man but almost never easy to decipher what he is doing. In other words, imagery is apprehensible, but symbolism or other meanings are more difficult to understand. This parallels the Hawaiian language in which double meanings are commonplace, and Hawaiian conversation, song, and dance are consistently enriched with at least two or three levels of possible interpretation.

The most common of the petroglyphs depicting the man image is the stick figure with head, torso, shoulders with arms hanging down, hips with legs in a standing posture. The figure is seldom geometrically perfect. Line is by far dominant over shape in both figure constructions and all other imagery. The variations on the man image found in Hawaii are almost endless. It would be useless to speculate on the meaning of all these different postures and configurations. There is a level at which some generalizations can be made: for example, a common variant is a figure with arms raised or with only one arm raised, or one foot and one arm raised; limbs which are apparently many-jointed would probably indicate movements such as walking, running, or dancing. An action of some sort is implied in all such cases, as with the figure holding a canoe paddle. The restrictions of the style, such as lineal frontality and a desire for simple clarity of images, result in some configurations that may not be what they seem on first view. The many pictures of men holding canoe paddles horizontally over the head are probably mere symbols for paddlers. The position shown is of no importance in itself—that is, it is not an illustration of that pose. It is obviously no accident that the figure has been so equipped, and no matter what the meaning at other possible levels of symbolism, at a level of representation the figure is easily apprehended and identified. The point is that we can recognize the action or activity in such examples, even if we do not know what they mean as action and activity. This class of petroglyphs should be identified as descriptive, since this function is self-evident and probably dominant.

Petroglyphs such as those in Figure 91 are found time and again in most known sites on all the Hawaiian Islands. The first figure emphasizes the maleness of the image, the second is obviously female, and the third is that of a child or baby. The man and woman image are self-evident in that the descriptive evidence is clear in the phallus, and the opening at the lower torso in the second figure. Since petroglyphs are created according to the physical appearance of the thing portrayed, the assumption is that the last figure is a child instead of being of less importance. In Egyptian art, where importance is signified by size, such a concept is abstract and consistent with the use of decorative elements as part of a design. An Egyptian looking at the above figures would say the small figure was unimportant, while a Hawaiian would simply say it was small. Since children are small it would, perforce, be a child.

Fig. 89. Runners
Puako, Hawaii, E3-1 (Kaeo trail)
Pohue Bay, Hawaii, B23-40

Fig. 90. Paddle-men
Puako, Hawaii, E3-1 (Paniau)

Fig. 91. Family (hypothetical)

Fig. 92.   Cryptic symbols
Various sites

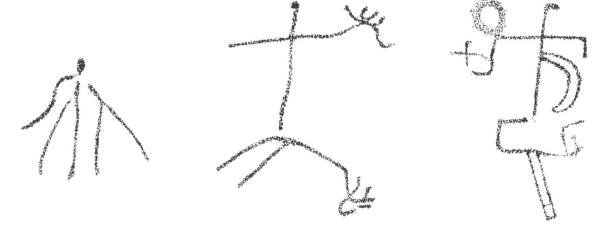

Fig. 93.   Enigmatic figures
Puako, Hawaii, E3-1

Another category among the figurative petroglyphs is the symbolic, for example, the figure which is ambiguously constructed or constructed in an unnatural manner. Figure 93 gives examples that are commonly found and for which there is no easy interpretation. We may assume purposefulness on the part of the carver since it would be impossible to create any of the above as one might create an image doodling with a pencil and paper. It must be remembered that these images were carved in rock with no corrective lines or erasures. Also, these are not isolated examples but frequent occurrences, which would suggest that there was some communication among the Hawaiians about the subject and meaning of such forms.

It is probable that cryptic petroglyphs will forever remain enigmatic. The above are a small sampling of the unusual and at times curious configurations which abound. In or out of context, there is no way to account for such a severe departure in imagery and subject from the descriptive and symbolic petroglyphs. Just as the symbolical group probably consists of personal and not general symbols, the cryptic group probably is the product of a very personal imagination. Just as the man image stands for a man, the cryptic images stand for themselves. Some could have been made simply for fun, for the joy of seeing a design take form—the realization of an act of creation. They mean what they were meant to mean by their creator and are no more apprehensible to an outsider than is the alphabet to an illiterate. It is almost certain that if they had meaning at all, it was a message for the select alone. Secret meanings, multiple meanings, and the use of symbolism were consistent with other practices within the Hawaiian culture.

These cryptic marks may be a parallel in the visual world to *kaona*, or hidden meanings and concealed references in poetry, chant, and legend. A similar equivocal treatment of elements occurs in tapa designing where the unit from which a design is constructed (the small bamboo stamp) is applied to the tapa surface in such a way that its true shape is obscured. This creates unexpected alignments of pattern, negative spaces may become positive, or new shapes may appear, while the source-shapes disappear and are known only to the designer.

That the petroglyphs were assigned meanings is indicated by the Ellis account (pages 31–32), although the information is meager and some of it open to question. It pretty well establishes the possibility of the use of the dot as a tally of men in the party and the circle as a symbol for trips. If this is indeed an intended system, the two elements express very neatly and with utmost simplicity the condition of the situation: the dot, a visually static mark symbolizing a thing in position—here; the curving line forming the circle is visually dynamic and refers to an action, which, however, is in the past, since the circle is closed. Two old Hawaiian informants supplied Beckwith (n.d.) with some meanings for specific petro-

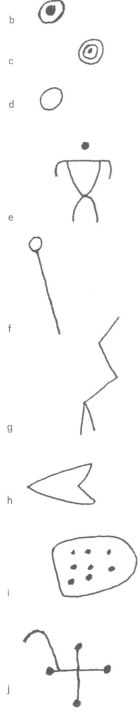

a

b

c

Fig. 94. Field sketches, Beckwith
Puuloa, Hawaii, HV-225

d

e

f

g

h

i

j

glyphs at Puuloa in 1915. They did not agree on all of them, but Beckwith's field notes contain the assigned meanings with sketches of the petroglyphs (Fig. 94). Two of these seem to be functional forms: (a) the hole for a child and (b) the hole for a first-born. In three cases the meanings are symbolic: (c) the first-born of an *ali'i*, (g) *mo'o* (lizard), and (i) family group, probably of an *ali'i*. Four others could be called representational: (d) *omaki* (*'umeke*—calabash, top view—for carrying *piko?),* (h) shark, (f) *pololu (pulo'ulo'u,* a *kapu* stick), (e) *akua* or *kanaka*, (j) cross borne before a chief at night in traveling. Men bear the ends—calabash hung on these ends, torch fastened on the bar. On the upright is affixed a Kalaipahoa (the name of a "poison" wood used in sorcery, or an image so used). The authenticity of such assignments as these in terms of ancient Hawaiian usage cannot be assessed at this time, but such reports serve to indicate that the petroglyphs fulfilled specific and seriously considered purposes of recording, communication, and ritual.

As there was no place for decoration in the man image (that is, each modification or addition to the basic stick figure had a descriptive purpose), to be consistent the same should be true for all petroglyphs. There is no reason to suppose that there would be totally different motives and attitudes for the construction of expressions which freely intermingle on the lava surfaces all through Hawaii. A thing is not decorative because it is not recognizable. Neither is a thing without meaning because it is not understood. It seems more than likely that petroglyphs were assigned meaning, and that this is true for all three categories; descriptive, symbolic, and cryptic. Material things were represented (as well as was practical within the style and technique), symbolical systems were used to depict acts and conditions, and cryptic or abstract images were used for secret and, possibly, ceremonial purposes.

The probable function of the *piko* tally marks at Puuloa and similar marks in other sites is fairly well established. Because of this and because of the great number of three

rticular kinds of these marks, a development from
nctionality to symbolism can be demonstrated. First,
ere is the simple *piko** hole, a circular depression in
e *pahoehoe* lava which averages 2 inches in diameter
d slightly less than 1 inch deep; second, the *piko* hole
th a circle incised around it; finally, a great number
variations on the theme of a central dot with variously
ncentric circles, fragments of circular or U shapes,
en such fragmented images as a series of dots
ich lie on the circumference of a circle, and bars
lines in series.

In the first case the simple *piko* hole is purely functional
container for the *piko*), with no aesthetic or obvious
mbolic overtones, although, as in Figure 31, it can
ggest a method of tally. In the second case the incising
a circle around it suggests that the *piko* hole may have
en invested with meaning (for example, Beckwith's
formant calls it a mark for a first-born child) as well as
nction. One may speculate on what the meaning is but
is is actually irrelevant to the point at hand. When, in the
ird case, the *piko* hole is merely symbolized by a dot and
surrounded by decorative embellishments, we have a
early complete object of art.

More specifically, a hole or receptacle in its most
imitive form may be absolutely utilitarian and have no
her values. This is the level at which bait cups and
pamu holes function. When there is a substitution of a
t for the hole, a symbol has been created. The

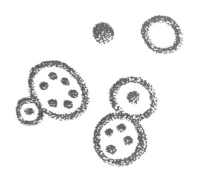

Fig. 95.   Circles with dots
Puuloa, Hawaii, HV-225

Fig. 96.   Family
Puuloa, Hawaii, HV-225

e word *piko* has more than one meaning. As a noun it refers to the navel,
vel string, and umbilical cord. Figuratively it can be used to refer to a
od relative and also to the genitals. It can be used to describe the summit
a hill, the crown of the head, tip of the ear, end of a rope, and the place
ere a leaf is attached to a stem. There are many other meanings as is
case with very many Hawaiian words.

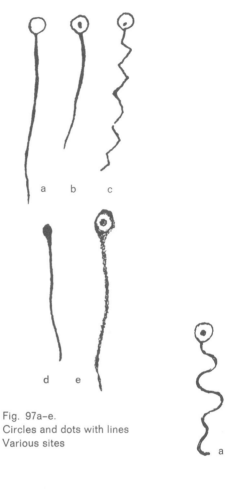

Fig. 97a–e.
Circles and dots with lines
Various sites

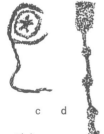

Fig. 98a–d.
Circles and dots with lines
Various sites

Fig. 99a–b. Twin symbols (?)
c. Triplet symbol (?)
Puuloa, Hawaii, HV-225

decorative embellishments surrounding the dot, dots, or lines connecting bars, are certainly of potential and often actual aesthetic value since they are of intrinsic interest. A multiplicity of dots in rows, groups, or contained within an enclosing shape would also suggest numbers (of people, trips, times, and so on). A group demonstrating the tally idea which is unmistakably composed as a unit is shown in Figure 96. With a previous knowledge of the symbolism at Puuloa, this probably is the record of a man, his wife, and a tally of their eleven children (possibly eight live children and three stillborn, or eight male and three female?).

Logical questions following a discussion of the development of a *piko* hole into a symbol are: why not use an old *piko* hole instead of creating a symbol?; and why create a symbol at all? There is no information about whether *piko* holes were ever used more than once. Considering the comparative ease of pecking a small hole into lava rock, and the sense of individuality which would urely result from having one's own *piko* hole, it seems unlikely that they were used more than once. The use of the symbol should not be surprising, since symbolical substitutions were fairly common in Hawaiian religion. All early accounts agree that an *akua* figure carved from wood could be symbolically invested with the *mana* of the god which it represented.

Why create a symbol at all? There would be no need for symbolical activity if it were possible or practical to carry out that action for which the symbol substitutes. A traveler visiting Puuloa without having saved the umbilical stump of a newly born, or those of already grown children, might make a symbol which would substitute for the act of burying the *piko*.

The petroglyphs at Puuloa may be divided into three categories: (1) the simple hole used for the placing of the *piko,* including the variants such as those functioning as a tally; (2) the anthropomorphic image, including both male and female figures ; (3) nonfigurative or cryptic symbols. The possible significance of the first category has been discussed, the second will be examined later, and the third here. Given that the nature of the petroglyphs at Puuloa shows a concern for birth and life-centered acts and possibly symbolic ones also, it seems appropriate to at least consider some of the apparently enigmatic petroglyph images as symbols related to birth, life, or both.

There are quite a few circles and dots with long trailing lines appearing in several distinct variations (Fig. 80). It is an interesting fact that these symbols occur almost exclusively on domed mounds or sloping pahoehoe and that the dot or circle is invariably above with the "tail" running down the slope. This symbol is not limited to the Puuloa site, but is fairly widespread on the island of Hawaii.

One interpretation, offered by Dr. Derrick B. Jelliffe,* is that the above could be a rather literal picture of the

placenta with the navel cord attached. According to Pukui (1942, p. 362) the placenta was always washed and either buried or deposited in a suitable place, one which would favorably influence the future life of the infant. Other placenta-like imagery at Puuloa is shown in Figure 98. On the other hand, Beckwith (n.d.) quotes an informant as saying that Figure 97 a represents a *pulo'ulo'u,* a staff with a tapa bundle on the top end, used as a sign of a *kapu* area.

Dr. Jelliffe remarked on the similarity between certain medical symbols and Figures 99 a, b, and c. Figure 99 a suggested to him a symbol for fraternal twins; Figure b a symbol for identical twins (where there would be one placenta but two umbilical cords); and Figure c, triplets. At least one informant refers to what amounted to a Caesarean operation, performed at Puuloa, where these symbols are found.

The images in Figures 97 and 98 all fit the pattern of a pancake-like shape with a trailing cord; this would be the simplest possible description for a placenta. Since there was ample opportunity for observation of the placenta, the umbilical cord, and the *piko* stump during the birth process, there is the possibility that Figures 98 b, c, and d were made as simplified naturalistic representations. In other words, some of the more cryptic symbols may not be symbols at all but attempts at simplified representation, as in the case of the human figures. This idea is proposed as a clearly speculative interpretation. However it seems possible that the circle and trailing line design is an extension of the *piko* mark and would carry an associated meaning. The two occur together at Puuloa where the circle-line symbol may have originated. The "birth scene" at Pakininui shown in Figure 64 a makes use of the *piko* motif on the two figures in the torso of the larger one, and the circle and trailing line symbol connected to the emerging figure, which does not have a *piko*. Being widely spread on the island (in Puna, Kau, South and North Kona, and South Kohala) the circle and line design is not likely to have been a private or local symbol, but instead served a common function in widely separated sites.

*Visiting Professor of Pediatrics, Children's Hospital, Honolulu, 1963. From University College, Makerere, Uganda, East Africa.

Myths and Legends

It is fortunate that a considerable number of the people who have been interested in the petroglyphs have had the opportunity to inquire about them from native Hawaiians. The accounts recorded range between ancient traditional history, legends, or myths, and explanations of why they were made, or stories about them which are often only vaguely remembered. Two of the explanatory type have already been related here—the Ellis account and Beckwith's information on the Puuloa site. These are the only two which seem to offer significant data of this kind. Others, more in the nature of traditional history or legend, are interesting enough in their own right to be retold here.

Stokes (1910, pp. 45–46), in reporting on the petroglyphs at Kahaluu, Kona, gives the following account:

At the time of these investigations there was living in Kahaluu an old native named Malanui, eighty-six years of age [born about 1823], who after the petroglyphs were marked led the writer to the beach and pointed out the figure of Kamalalawalu. [A large, deeply cut, headless figure on the beach shelf, under water at high tide.] The other petroglyphs, when his attention was called to them, he declared he knew nothing of, and offered no suggestions. The following bit of history had been previously communicated by him, and is confirmed in part by Fornander [1880, Vol. 2, p. 123].

When Kamalalawalu, king of Maui, invaded Hawaii, Lonoikamakahiki the king of Hawaii [about 1600 according to traditional genealogies] was in Kahaluu. On hearing of the landing near Kawaihae bay, Lono held a council of war at which two old priests presented the following plan: Lono was to disgrace them and drive them from court; they were to seek refuge from the enemy and confidence being gained advice was to be given that a march be made inland toward Waimea where they were to claim that Lono was in such a weak position that his defeat was certain. The plot succeeded, and while Kamalalawalu marched inland, Lono brought his forces along the coast from Kahaluu and cut off the retreat. Kamalalawalu was killed in the engagement that ensued. His body was brought to Kahaluu, a picture made of it on the rock, and the body sacrificed in the nearby *heiau* [temple] of Keeku.

This account may very well be actual history, including the making of the petroglyph. The following, however, is strictly a myth, although it may have been believed by some of its narrators.

Fig. 100. A line of marching men at Paniau (HA-E3-1). See figure 60 for detail of large figures at the end of the line.

The demigod Niheu, second son of the goddess Hina, was fishing in the waters near Kalapana. When he threw in his hook a little *pao'o* caught his bait but he could not land it. When he pulled in the hook the fish flew away. The *pao'o* was also a *kupua*—a supernatural being—as was Niheu. Since Niheu could not catch the *pao'o* and was not getting any other fish either, he went to a prophetess who told him he would get no fish until he had killed the *pao'o*. He went out at night with torches to try to lure the fish but without success. He tried to catch it in his net but when he thought he had the *pao'o,* it turned out to be some other fish. The fish could fly through the air faster than Niheu could follow. Once when Niheu was after it, it flew to the crater of Napau at Kilauea and then to the spot called Aikua near the Wahaula *heiau.* As Niheu threw his spear at the *pao'o* he stepped in the *pahoehoe* and left his footprint there. But the spear did not hit the fish because a plover cried out just as the spear was thrown and warned the *pao'o,* which dived down a hole in the lava and leaped into the sea. The spear landed, too late, in the hole where the *pao'o* had disappeared.

The footprint is there, a petroglyph made in the well-worn path south of the *heiau,* with a number of other symbols, dots, and a figure of a man (Niheu?). The hole of the *pao'o,* a small tree-mold, made as the lava burned out a small tree, is alongside the trail nearby. They say the type of *pao'o* (a small goby) in the Kalapana waters is the *pao'o kauila* and is a little different from the kinds found in other places.

Niheu's exploits and feats of prowess, usually more successful than this one, are told with numerous variations throughout the islands. The above version is compiled from several accounts given by the natives of Kalapana. The petroglyph of the footprint and the other symbols may have been made as a kind of illustration of this Niheu story, but it is more likely that the local versions of the tale were adjusted to include the natural tree-mold hole and drawings that were made for other purposes. In any case it is a good example, though these are rare, of local traditions relating closely to petroglyphs.

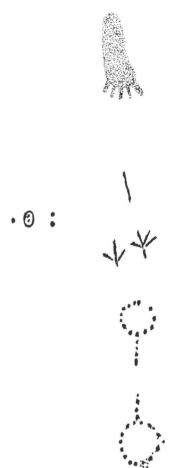

Fig. 101. Niheu's footprint
Puna, Hawaii, HV-297

The Moanalua site, toward the head of Moanalua Valley on Oahu, is a large boulder covered with petroglyphs, known by the name of *Pohaku-ka-luahine* (the old woman's stone). McAllister (1933, p. 100) collected a current tradition about it:

During the consecration of a *heiau* in Moanalua Valley, a small child cried. Now, any noise made by man or animal during such apu periods meant instant death for the offender. The grandmother, desiring to protect the child, ran with it up the valley and hid behind this rock. Men were sent out in search, but were unable to find them. After the elapse of the tapu period of a few days the woman and the child were safe and returned to their home. Namakahelu, the oldest living kamaaina [native born] of Moanalua Valley, is of the opinion this is a recent story. The stone, she says, was sacred, an *akua* [god] with at least two forms of which she knows. As a stone it was known as Laupo, and as a bird it was known as Laea. Offerings were placed before it.

Unfortunately this reveals nothing about the petroglyphs themselves nor their origin or meaning, and seems to indicate that the informants had no knowledge of, or interest in them, but only in the significance of the rock itself. Two of the figures on the rock have bird-like heads and arms that suggest wings. The small symbol between the curved legs of the larger bird figure is curiously like a child. Is this the grandmother and child? The bird-god Laea? Or both? Or is it another instance of a birth scene?

On the slopes above Moomomi Bay on the north shore of Molokai the ancient trail crosses a stretch of air-formed sandstone, sand blown up from the dunes below and hardened by weathering. Near the trail are *Kalaina wawae* (Kalaina's feet), several score of box-like depressions cut into the sandstone surface. A local story relates that the custom of making these marks was started by Kalaina, a prophetess of Moomomi. One day she went to the trail and made two hollows in the sandstone. On the next day she called all the people to the place and proclaimed that someday people with feet like these would come from the sea, thereby prophesying the arrival of the boot-wearing Caucasians. Ever since, the practice of making "footprints" here has been carried on by travelers who have passed this way on the trail. John Stokes, who recorded this story

prior to 1909, observed that most of the prints are merely oblong depressions, not particularly like a footprint but in the general size and proportion of one. Only four of the group have toe marks, in contrast to the usual petroglyph of a footprint which has the toes clearly indicated. Some of the depressions at Moomomi are as deep as two inches and one has a more deeply cut section suggesting the heel of a boot.

There is another story that features petroglyphs of footprints: At the Lualailua Hills, on the southern slopes of Haleakala, Maui, there is a small patch of *pahoehoe* with about thirty small footprints carved into it. On inquiring about the possible origin of these, after a visit to the site with Joseph Marciel in 1922, Kenneth Emory reported that he was told they were made by the *Menehune** while carrying stones to build the *heiau* at Loaloa at Kaupo, which is about 13 miles to the east. The stones were so heavy that the bearers' feet sank into the lava as they crossed this area. There are a number of cases of natives claiming that petroglyphs are the work of the *Menehune*. It is a ready solution and is applied quite freely to explain many archaeological features.

Two traditions relating to the petroglyphs on the eight boulders on the south bank of the Wailua River in Kauai (Site KA, A1-6) are reported in the Hawaiian Historical Society Report for 1916. One of these related that these rocks are the eight brothers of the demigod Maui.

Maui wished to bring the Hawaiian Islands together and for that purpose to catch the powerful fish Luehu, which if he hooked, would cause all the islands to draw together. The fish could only be caught on the night of Lono and Maui would go out on that night each month with his eight brothers to fish for it. . . . His mother, Hina, told him not to disturb any bailing dish he might find floating in the water at the mouth of Wailua River, as this would be his beautiful sister, Hina-ke-kaa. However, when Maui saw a dish for bailing out canoes floating near he told his brothers not to look behind them on pain of death and picked up the

*"Legendary race of small people who worked at night, building fishponds, roads, temples; if the work was not finished in one night, it remained unfinished." (Pukui and Elbert, 1957)

bailing dish and put it behind him in the canoe, where it turned into a beautiful woman. As soon as Luehu was caught the Hawaiian Islands began to draw together. As Kauai and Oahu came near great crowds gathered on the shores of Oahu and cheered. This did not disturb the brothers of Maui at first, who paddled steadily, but when the cheerers exclaimed at the beauty of the woman behind Maui, all the brothers turned at once to look. Immediately the great fish became loose from the hook and the islands slid apart. . . . Because of their looking back Maui's brothers were, on their return to Wailua, turned into stones and set across the mouth of the Wailua River.

In this same report there is brief reference to another story about these petroglyphs:

They are said to have formed part of the wall of the City of Refuge when the course of the river was different. They are called "Pae-mahu-o-Wailua," also *paikii*, or picture rocks. It is said that a sculptor of ancient times, carving idols, could only make one to suit him and threw the others away. These rocks are some of them, the marks being the hieroglyphics of the ancient sculptor.

The occurrence of the beautifully executed petroglyphs of dogs at the Nuuanu Valley site (Fig. 6) has led to speculation that they may be representations of Kaupe, the legendary ghost dog of Nuuanu. He was said to haunt the *pali* trail and to see him meant sudden disaster for the traveler. If the pictures are of Kaupe, they may have been made as an appeal to him for assistance, or a warning of his ghostly presence, or as part of a ritual to insure safe passage for the traveler.

Other than these few instances of tales and legends about known petroglyphs, there is little on record that connects any specific ones to Hawaiian traditional history. There are a few other accounts of inquiries having been made of natives, but the answers have not been particularly significant in filling out the total picture of the petroglyphs. One must conclude—as also seems true in other places where petroglyphs occur—that they were a somewhat obscure and specialized activity, having only a local, and usually temporary impact on the communal mind.

Fig. 102.   Bird-head figures, Moanalua, Oahu, A7-1

The Petroglyphs as Art

The contemplation of a work of art involves a highly complex set of reactions which are difficult to define and for which explanations and systems have never been very satisfactory. When the work is from a culture other than our own there will almost certainly be further complications and limitations in understanding. In viewing the Hawaiian petroglyphs, at least four possible points of view may be taken, each requiring a different cognition and a different type of awareness.

(1) We may consider what they represent to us as images, the subject matter, what ideas they suggest, or what they seem to symbolize. We can do this without knowledge of the Hawaiian culture. It is the first level of reaction, obvious and easily knowable, but of no great significance in itself.

(2) We may react to and judge what they are to us as design, expression, or decoration, or what they reveal as technical achievement, examples of creative inventiveness, or other aesthetic qualities which reside in the visual elements themselves. This requires no reference to meanings, or representations from our culture or the Hawaiian culture; moreover, to react purely to these values, which are intrinsic to the objects, it is necessary to avoid references to the culture which produced them. This second response to the petroglyphs, presupposing a special type of awareness, will be less sharply defined and possibly more difficult to achieve, but is likely to be more rewarding than the first.

(3) We may recognize what they were to the Hawaiians as subject matter, ideas, or symbols. This becomes more difficult because some prior knowledge of Hawaiian culture is necessary if we are to recognize the connotations intended by the makers. Even with the considerable knowledge available about the ancient Hawaiian culture, a great amount of the content of the petroglyphs remains an enigma. These meanings, symbols, and representations from inside the Hawaiian world will very likely be different from those which might be supplied from outside the culture. This content is supplied from sources that are actually outside the petroglyphs themselves; it could and did exist in other media, in verbal or narrative form, without reference to the petroglyphs. Even if the precise meanings of many of the petroglyphs are not clear, the subjects are generally recognizable except in those abstract or cryptic forms which must remain undeciphered unless new information becomes available. Does their enigmatic quality mean they were symbols which were secret, or limited to a few individuals, or to a family, possibly relating to magic or esoteric beliefs that were not to be divulged? Since a simple form, such as a circle, can have a number of meanings, might some of them represent just a one-time reference in the mind of the maker, an idea known only to him and intending no communication beyond this? Or were their meanings once common knowledge, or possibly local knowledge, which failed to be passed along into historic times?

(4) We may also consider what the petroglyphs were to the Hawaiian in terms of aesthetics as design, decoration, expression, or other related qualities. As to how the Hawaiians may have reacted to the purely visual aspects of the forms, there is simply no information. Judgments on this, based on references from our own culture are not likely to be useful—if they are not actually misleading. Apparently, to the Hawaiian, concepts which we call aesthetics were not structured or verbalized. Whatever reactions there were to the qualities of the visual elements, they were probably not separated out as a special content of an event, but were simply felt as part of what one saw—as common as the simple enjoyment of such things as humor, or good food. We also do not know what values, if any, the Hawaiians may have assigned to the refinement of techniques of making the petroglyphs, or whether they valued the apparent imaginative and creative qualities, or whether there was any notion that the "better" petroglyph makers were thought of as "artists." There is no way of knowing the ability of the average Hawaiian as an image maker; but many of the petroglyphs show a degree of inventiveness, design sense, and over-all evocative quality that can hardly be attributed to average talent. If it was partly the intention of any of the petroglyph

makers to provide a pleasant or visually rewarding arrangement of forms, then we may say that the images were functioning (in that context) as an art. As evidenced from their sculpture and tapa design, the Hawaiians clearly had the ability and obviously the intention to enhance these objects beyond the simple needs of function. Is it reasonable to expect that similar intentions would be practiced by some of the petroglyph makers? At present it is possible to fill in these unknowables (and only in a very tentative way) to the extent that we may assume the Hawaiian concepts of art were reasonably equivalent to our own.

Regardless of what the Hawaiians had in mind, the petroglyphs may be observed from within the framework of our own art values. To avoid misinterpretation this had best be done on the level of the "pure" visual intuitive response to line, shape, color, texture, pattern, and organization of elements. However, associated fringe benefits are bound to occur, since the images will also communicate in terms of anecdotes, symbols, and ideas seemingly inherent in our consciousness when we are confronted with representations of the human figure; and we cannot avoid assigning vague but pervasive meanings to the primary abstract symbols which are basic to man. The admittedly crude and unsophisticated quality of some of the petroglyphs, rather than distracting from the richness of the visual effect, may very well be the source of the intensity of our response. They are expressive in this way as a residue of simple human actions, direct and unencumbered by extraneous restraints. The fragmentary and cryptic quality of much of the imagery allows for the full play of the viewer's imagination. Participation in completing the imagery on his own terms brings to the viewer a sense of creation—an identification of the observer with the intent of the maker.

We note that the Hawaiian petroglyph style has a surprisingly wide range of variation, with each type offering a different quality of expression. Some are rugged and coarse, some refined and graceful, some rigidly static, others active. Gesture and articulation are often charming or humorous. We readily admire the direct and penetrating insight by which the designer seemed to choose just the right element to describe an object or action. No doubt most petroglyph enthusiasts have only the vaguest notion of the source of their interest, but it is fairly certain that a good part of it comes from the visual relationship of patterns, textures, and lines, the sense of the presence of a creative process, the mystery evoked by an unknown past, and the numerous associations that invariably accompany these experiences.

In our consideration of the most significant aspect of the petroglyphs, that is, their value as documents of Hawaiian history and culture, attention should be given to both objective and subjective evaluations. Information and conclusions can be developed from systematic recording, measurement, and imaginative analysis in a variety of ways. These are the bases of factual knowledge. Full understanding, however, requires also some attention to the less tangible dimensions that resist classification and are not easily grasped conceptually, the kind of content that is not measured but felt, not reasoned but intuited, those qualities that are inherent in even the simplest expressions of the creative spirit.

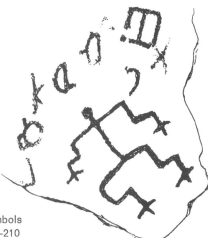

Fig. 103. Figure, symbols
Kamooalii, Hawaii, HV-210

A List of Petroglyph Sites in the Hawaiian Islands

All the sites presently recorded on each of the islands are listed here. In almost all cases the site names are merely those of the *ahupua'a,* or of a geographical feature such as a gulch, hill, or beach, followed by an area or district designation. Except in very rare instances they are not likely to be the names given to the petroglyph places by the ancient Hawaiians. The Hawaiian names for the sites have very rarely been recorded. The site numbers given are established by Bishop Museum as a control for recording site information, and to provide an index for filing field notes, photographs, and other pertinent data. The listing also includes a brief description of the kind of site, its location, an indication of the type of petroglyphs found there, and an estimate of the number of units. In most cases, the number of units is a very rough estimate, since a count is seldom possible. Regrettably, the location descriptions are not complete enough to be very useful guides for the petroglyph hunter. Complete and accurate location descriptions would become impossibly long and involved. Longitude and latitude coordinates are available from the Bishop Museum records, but these are omitted here because they are useful mainly to locate the sites on a standardized map and are not very useful in the field. For those persons interested in finding the petroglyph areas, local residents and landowners are the best source of information. Since many of the sites are on private property, permission to search (or informing the owner of intentions) is advised. The listed references indicate sources of information on the sites. The complete titles for these references will be found in the bibliography.

Fig. 104. Paddle-man
Puako, Hawaii, E3-1

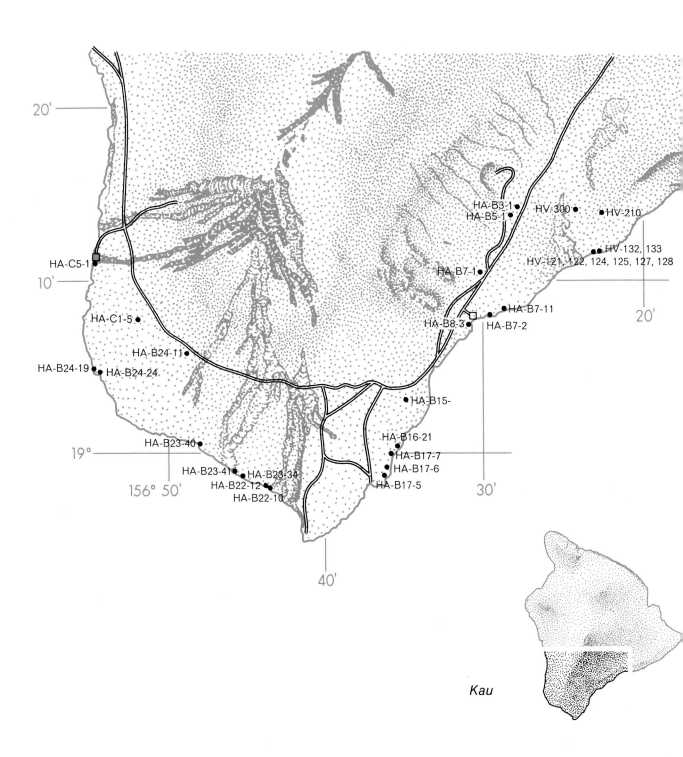

20'

HA-B3-1 •
HA-B5-1 •

HV-300 •

HV-210 •

HV-132, 133 •
HV-121, 122, 124, 125, 127, 128 •

HA-C5-1 ☐

10'

HA-B7-1 •

HA-C1-5 •

HA-B7-11 •

HA-B8-3 ☐   HA-B7-2 •

20'

HA-B24-11 •

HA-B24-19 •   HA-B24-24 •

HA-B15- •

HA-B16-21 •

HA-B23-40 •

19°

HA-B17-7 •
HA-B17-6 •

30'

HA-B23-41 •   HA-B23-34 •
156° 50'   HA-B22-12 •
HA-B22-10 •

HA-B17-5 •

40'

Kau

Kaukulau, Puna   HA-A12-1
    Near Lilioa Point, southern boundary of Kaukalua
    and Malamaki, on *pahoehoe*.
    Circles—figures—lines overlaid.

Kapapala Cave, Kapapala Ranch,
Kaalaala-Makakupu, Kau   HA-B3-1
    4 miles N.N.E. of Pahala,
    ½ mile east of Highway #11.
    Human figures.
    ±20 units.
    Baker (1922). p. 53 ("Cave of Refuge"?)

Turtle Cave, Kauhuhuula, Kau   HA-B5-1
    2½ miles N.N.E. of Pahala between Wood Valley
    road and Volcano Highway, in Piikea Gulch.
    Line of human figures at entrance.
    Human figures (crude) on "Turtle Back," inside cave.
    ±60 units.
    Baker (1922). p. 54.

Moalua Cave, Moalua, Kau   HA-B7-1
    ½ mile inland from Volcano Road, in Moalua Gulch.
    Lineal human figures and parts.
    ±20 units.
    Judd (1904), p. 190 (describes 3 caves as being 1 mile
    mauka of mill, about 5 miles from the sea, directly
    inland from hill, "Kameha.")

Moaula Kopu Mahaka, Kau   HA-B7-2
    3,400 feet west of Kamehame Hill on the sides of a
    faint trail going north. An area of about 60 x 60 feet
    near an *ahu* (cairn).
    Linear figures, angular diagrams.
    ±50 units.
    Stokes (1910), p. 276 (?).
    V. Hansen. Kau folder, B.P.B.M.

Moaula Kopu Mahaka, Kau   HA-B7-11
    About ½ mile east of Punaluu Bay and ½ mile north
    of site B7-10 (on the coast). The area has been
    disturbed by bulldozer making water holes.
    Some petroglyphs covered by soil and grass.
    Curved linear figures, angular diagrams, footprint.
    V. Hansen. Kau folder, B.P.B.M.

Punaluu, Kau   HA-B8-3
    Along low lava shore between Ninole and Punaluu
    village.
    Linear human figures, curved arms and legs, family
    groups—fish(?)—dots—circles.
    ±25 units.
    Stokes (1910), p. 276 (illus.).

Naalehu, Kawala, Kau   HA-B15-
    A cave shelter approximately 2 miles from shore,
    on trail from Naalehu to south.
    Lineal human figures.
    ±15 units.
    Westervelt (1906), pp. 164–169.
    Stokes (1910), p. 275 (illus.).
    Baker (1922), p. 53.

Kahilipali Point, Kahilipalinui, Kau   HA-B16-21
    On coarse *pahoehoe*, near coastal trail at
    Kahilipali Point.
    Lineal human figures—dots—*papamu*—footprints—
    turtle—various abstractions.
    ±75 units.
    V. Hansen. Kau folder, B.P.B.M.

Kamilo, Waiohinu, Kau   HA-B17-5
    Approximately ½ mile north of Lae-o-Kamilo on rough
    pahoehoe, near coast trail, coarse surface.
    Lineal and rectangular human figures—*papamu*, some
    deeply cut, eroded.
    ±30 units.
    V. Hansen. Kau folder, B.P.B.M.

Keoneokahuku, Waiohinu, Kau   HA-B17-6
    Approximately 1 mile north of Lae-o-Kamilo (approx.
    ½ mile north of B17-5) on rough *pahoehoe*, near
    coast trail, coarse surface.
    Lineal figures, variety of shapes.
    ±50 units.
    V. Hansen. Kau folder, B.P.B.M.

Kii, Waiohinu, Kau   HA-B17-7
    Approximately 1½ miles north of Lae-o-Kamilo on
    rough *pahoehoe*, near coast trail.
    Open torso, angular, and profile human figures.
    ±50 units.
    V. Hansen. Kau folder, B.P.B.M.

Kahio, Pakininui, Kau   HA-B22-10
    At Hawea, on *pahoehoe*.
    Human figures, lineal and open triangular (two figures
    inside large triangular torso and one at pelvis with
    circle and trailing line symbol attached)—small
    papamu—lettering.
    ±10 units.
    V. Hansen. Kau folder, B.P.B.M.

Pakininui, Kau   HA-B22-12

On *pahoehoe,* just west of 1868 *aa* flow (approximately ½ mile west of B22-10).
Lineal and triangular human figures.
±10 units.
V. Hansen. Kau folder, B.P.B.M.

Hopeloa, Kahuku, Kau   HA-B23-34

On slanting *pahoehoe,* near shelter caves, ¼ mile from Kau edge of 1887 flow, near coast trail.
3 human figures.
V. Hansen photo. Kau folder, B.P.B.M.

Pohue Bay, Kahuku, Kau   HA-B23-40

On *pahoehoe,* inland and east from sandy beach, and on trail toward east (north of cinder cone) at edge of depression, also, west of bay.
Wide variety.
Figures—dots—circles—abstractions—fan—crabs—ships—rubbing holes—dates—names.
Several hundred units.
Cox. Field notes. B.P.B.M.

Kahakahakea, Kahuku, Kau   HA-B23-41

Approximately 3 miles S.E. of Pohue Bay, on coastal trail, ¾ mile N.W. of Hopeloa.
A few human figures, lettering.

Kahiawai, Manuka, Kau   HA-B24-11

At Kahiawai, near triangulation station, near east boundary of Manuka, below highway.
Lettering (one unit)—overlapping lines—circles—figures, etc.

Manuka Bay, Manuka, Kau   HA-B24-19

On north shore of bay just east of the Manuka-Kaulanamauna boundary.
Lettering.
3-4 units.

Kipuka Malua, Manuka, Kau   HA-B24-24

One mile south of Manuka Bay.
Human figure (open torso—eight dots across the shoulders).

Milolii, South Kona   HA-C5-1

Beyond end of road, south of the village, scattered.
Circles—dots—*papamu*—a few figures—grinding cups (circle with 18 concentric lines).
±20 units.
Cox. Field notes. B.P.B.M. 1966.

Kaulanamauna, South Kona   HA-C1-5

On lava slabs in paved trail (Site C1-1) approximately 1 mile below Highway 11 (at 1,200 ft. elevation) and approximately ¼ mile on the Kona side of the jeep trail to the shore.
V. Hansen. Field notes.

Honaunau, South Kona   HA-C15-20

In City of Refuge National Historical Park, widely scattered on flat and hillside.
Human figures—abstract symbols—*papamu* near shore.
±125 units.
Touhy (1965).

Keei (1), South Kona   HA-C21-3

On *pahoehoe* ledge at the shore, ½ mile south of Kealakekua Bay, at Kahiwawai Harbor.
Large abstract geometric figures (Stokes thought they might not be Hawaiian. Cut with steel tools?).
5 units.
Stokes. MS. notes. (Illus.) B.P.B.M.

Kaawaloa, South Kona   HA-C23-210

About 100 yards northeast of Puhina-o-Lono *heiau,* on road to Kaawaloa flat from Captain Cook.
Several human figures.
Soehren and Newman (1968), pp. 16–17.

Keauhou, North Kona   HA-D3-7

Approximately at center of Kuamoo battlefield, approximately ¼ mile south of Keauhou Bay.
Slanted *pahoehoe* rise, Kuamoo battlefield.
Circles—dots—lines—some names near trail.
±20 units.
Cox. Field notes. B.P.B.M.

Kahaluu, North Kona   HA-D4-4

On shore and under water, a few yards south of Keeku *heiau.*
Figures, several kinds and sizes.
Sculptured relief (Kamalalawalu legend).
±15 units.
Stokes (1910), pp. 259–273 (illus.).

Holualoa (4), North Kona   HA-D6-1

In Keolononihi *heiau* enclosure at Kamoa Point, on two boulders.
Crude diagrams (figures?).
2-4 units.

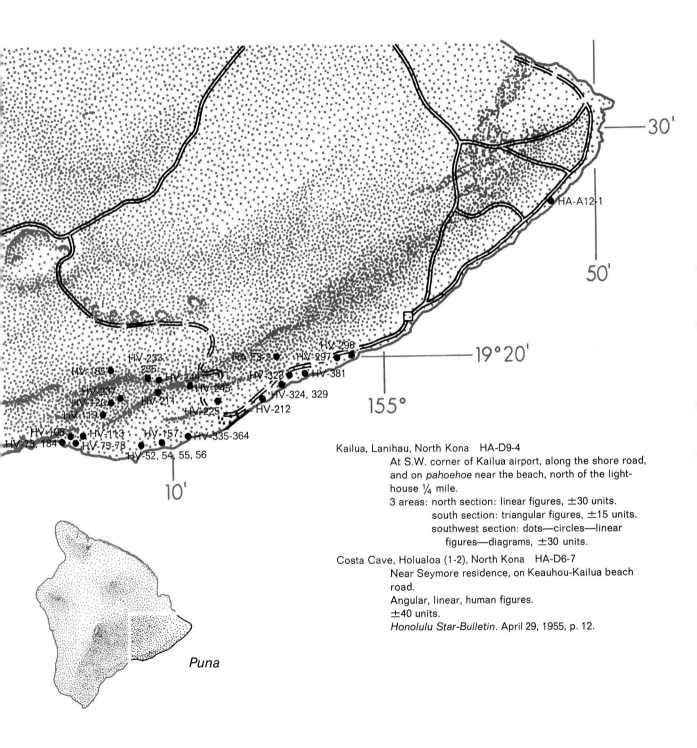

HV-298
HA-F3-2 • HV-297
HV-233 HV-233
HV-185 235 HV-323 • HV-381
HV-237 HV-244 HV-324, 329
HV-120 HV-211 HV-245 HV-212
HV-119 HV-225
HV-108 HV-113 HV-157 HV-335-364
HV-73, 184 HV-75-78
HV-52, 54, 55, 56

30'

50'

19°20'

155°

10'

HA-A12-1

Puna

Kailua, Lanihau, North Kona   HA-D9-4
    At S.W. corner of Kailua airport, along the shore road,
    and on *pahoehoe* near the beach, north of the light-
    house ¼ mile.
    3 areas: north section: linear figures, ±30 units.
              south section: triangular figures, ±15 units.
              southwest section: dots—circles—linear
                  figures—diagrams, ±30 units.

Costa Cave, Holualoa (1-2), North Kona   HA-D6-7
    Near Seymore residence, on Keauhou-Kailua beach
    road.
    Angular, linear, human figures.
    ±40 units.
    Honolulu Star-Bulletin. April 29, 1955, p. 12.

Honokohau, North Kona   HA-D12-3
   At concrete salt pans.
   2 *papamu*—full-rigged ship—footprints.
   (Baker's photos show guns—triangular figures).
   Baker (1919), pp. 131–135 (illus.).
   Soehren (1963a).

Honokohau, North Kona   HA-D12-13
   South of Aimakapa Pond.
   Linear figures—paddle-man—letters—multiple
   limbed figure.
   Baker (1919), pp. 131–135 (illus.).
   Soehren (1963a).

Kaloko, North Kona   HA-D13-13
   On coast trail, south of Kaloko Pond.
   Linear figures with curved arms and legs—
   gourd helmet (?).
   ±12 units.
   Soehren (1963a).

Kalolo, North Kona   HA-D19-1
   On coastal trail.
   Lettering.

Kaupulehu, North Kona   HA-D22-19, 22, 23
   D22-19: On *pahoehoe*, east of pond,
         mauka of *kiawe* grove.
   D22-22: ½ mile inland from pond,
         adjacent to 1801 lava flow.
   D22-23: 1 mile(?), inland, adjacent to 1801 lava flow.
   Sails—figures with elaborate headdresses—paddle-
   men—*papamu*—turtle-men carrying human on pole
   (sacrifice ?).
   ±85 units—indefinite number under *kiawe* growth.
   Soehren (1963a), pp. 28, 30.

North and South Kona

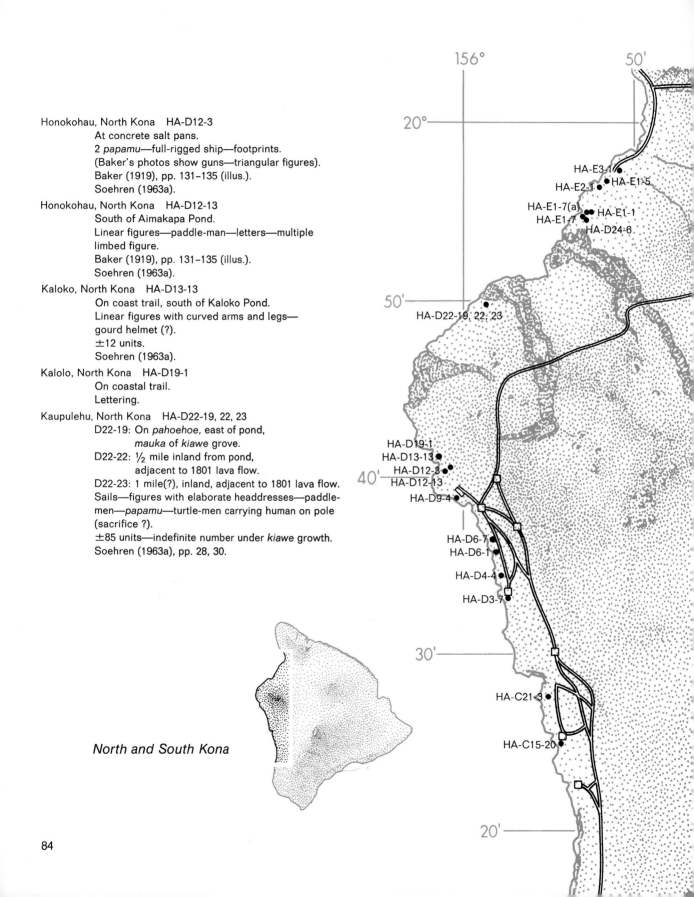

apalaoa, Puuanahulu, North Kona   HA-D24-6
   At northern edge of Puuanahulu, on *pahoehoe*
   near shore.
   Ships—figures—guns—horse—lettering—feet
   (sandals?)—fishhooks.

aluamanini   HA-(no number)
   Midway between Anaehoomalu beach and Kapalaoa
   about 100 yards inland on *pahoehoe* around opening
   of a large cave.
   Human figures, triangular, linear and relief.
   ±75 units.

naehoomalu, South Kohala   HA-E1-1
   On coastal trail from Puako, on border between
   Anaehoomalu and Waikoloa, at southern edge of
   aa flow.
   A great variety of human figures—circles—
   abstractions.
   About two acres.
   Several thousand units.
   Stokes (1910), p. 279 (Puuanahulu).
   Baker (1919), pp. 131–135.
   Bryan (1951), pp. 8–9.

alahuipuaa, Lahuipu, South Kohala   HA-E1-5
   ¼ mile inland from Manoku fishpond, near Kiholo-
   Puako trail, at cave site H-100.
   Linear and triangular human figures—dots—circles—
   papamu.
   ±100 units.

naehoomalu-kai, South Kohala   HA-E1-7(a)
   About ¼ mile inland, between Site E1-1 and
   Anaehoomalu Bay.
   Triangular human figures—diagrams—chickens—
   circles—dots.

naehoomalu Beach, South Kohala   HA-E1-7
   On *pahoehoe* beach shelf, sometimes under sand.
   Repeated wavy lines (possibly not petroglyphs)—
   papamu—figure.
   Stokes (1910), p. 279 (Puuanahulu).
   Baker (1919), pp. 131–135.
   Bryan (1951), pp. 8–9.

apakonane, Waikoloa, South Kohala   HA-E2-1
   ½ mile east (inland from) Papakonane boat landing,
   Pauoa Bay.
   Linear figures—feet (or sandals)—fishhooks.
   ±20 units.

Puako, Lalamilo, South Kohala   HA-E3-1
   Paniau. On *pahoehoe* and rough lava. Approximately
   ½ mile south of Kapaniau Point, and
   200–500 feet inland.
   Linear figures—line of marchers—large
   "Lono" figure—paddles.
   Kaeo Trail. Approximately ½ mile from Paniau sites,
   on *pahoehoe*. Heavy concentration.
   Linear figures—family groups. Also,
   scattered along Kaeo Trail to the north,
   triangular human figures—muscular figures—
   sails.
   ±3,000 units.
   Baker (1920), pp. 49–52.
   B.P.B.M. (1964) (Puako Report).
   Emory (1956a).
      (1956b), pp. 9–11.

Puako Shore, South Kohala   HA-E-(no number)
   On *pahoehoe* at the shore at end of right-of-way
   to the beach from Puako Road, south side of No. 152,
   opposite right-of-way to Puako petroglyphs (Site E3-1).
   Human figures, spiked headdress, *papamu*.
   ±15 units.

Puu Ulaula, Kalala, North Kohala   HA-F3-2
   On boulders on south summit of Puu Ulaula (Red Hill)
   on the coast approximately 4¼ miles N.W. of
   Kawaihae.
   Linear angular human figures, some retouched or
   recently made.
   ±10 units.

Panau Trail, Laeapuki-Kamoamoa, Puna   HV-(no number)
   At 351 feet elevation bench mark on Panau Trail from
   Kalapana to Chain of Craters, at boundary between
   the two *ahupua'a*.
   Human figures—lettering.
   ±4 units.
   Emory, Cox, and Others (1959), p. 92.

Apua, Puna   HV-52, 54, 55, 56
   Several groups on *pahoehoe* just north of a large
   collapsed tumulus, ½ mile N.E. of Apua Point.
   Human figures.
   ±50 units.
   Emory, Ladd, Soehren (1965), pp. 151, 152, 154.
   Map XII A, B.

Halape, Kapapala, Kau   HV-73, 184
  On *pahoehoe*, between shore and deep crack,
  inland and east of Halape cabin.
  Human figures.
  ±20 units.
  Emory, Ladd, Soehren (1965), p. 82. Map IV.

Keauhou, Kau   HV-75-78
  Approximately 1 mile west of Halape, between fault
  zone and sea. Two caves, 500 yards east of bluff,
  west of Keauhou Bay, also east of landing near shore.
  Human figures, circles, abstract symbols.
  75–100 units.
  Hudson. ms. 1931. pp. 508–514.
  Emory. ms. 1949, 1961.
  Emory, Ladd, Soehren (1965), p. 29, Map V, Fig. 7, 17,
  Pl. IB, IIA, B.
  Emory, Cox, and Others (1959), pp. 108, 109.

Keauhou, Kau   HV-108
  A cave, 1,000 feet N.W. from HV-75, just above bluff
  and fault zone.
  Several petroglyphs on walls of cave.
  Emory, Ladd, Soehren (1965), p. 65.
  Map V. Pl. I B, II A, B.

Keauhou, Kau   HV-113
  On large slab of *pahoehoe* around edge of collapsed
  lava tube. 1,400 feet N.N.E. from HV-75.
  Several large petroglyphs, triangular- and columnar-
  bodied figures.
  Emory, Ladd, Soehren (1965), p. 67. Map V, Pl. III B.

Keauhou Inland, Keauhou, Kau   HV-119
  On very edge of Holei Pali, overlooking Keauhou,
  approximately 1½ miles inland, and ¼ mile east of
  the Keauhou-Apua boundary, outside of a cave
  entrance.
  Lineal human figures—circles—lettering.
  Emory, Ladd, Soehren (1965), p. 69.
  Smart. Field Notes Hawaii Volcano Reports.

Apua Inland, Apua, Puna   HV-120
  On walls of break-in at a lava tube shelter, between
  Poliokeawe Pali and Holei Pali (2½ miles inland) 600
  feet east of Kau-Puna boundary.
  Human figures, simple triangular.
  Emory, Ladd, Soehren (1965), p. 69.

Kuee Village, Kapapala, Kau   HV-121, 122, 124, 125, 127, 128
  At Kuee village ruins, about 10 miles east of Punaluu,
  on Pahala-Kuee Trail, scattered throughout village
  site.
  Human figures—canoes—*papamu.*
  17 units at site 125.
  Emory, Ladd, Soehren (1965), pp. 69-71.
  Map I. Fig. 20A, 21.

Kuee, Kapapala, Kau   HV-132, 133
  On top of cliff, ¼ mile east of Kuee village. Site 132,
  inland of trail. Site 133 on sea side of trail, near edge
  of cliff at shore line.
  Several human figures.
  Emory, Ladd, Soehren (1965), p. 72.

Kahue, Puna   HV-157
  One mile west of Kealakomo, on shore trail on
  slanted *pahoehoe*, at edge of depression which
  surrounds well. ("Mrs. Riley's place")
  Lines—*papamu*—circles.
  ±6 units.
  Emory, Cox, and Others (1959), p. 106.
  Emory, Ladd, Soehren (1965), p. 77.

Apua Upland, Apua, Puna   HV-185
  ¼ mile west of Keauhou-Apua boundary, 4/5 mile
  above Poliokeawe Pali.
  Human figures—twin paddle-men.
  ±30 units.
  Emory, Ladd, Soehren (1965), p. 83.
  Smart (1965), Fig. 20B. Pl. IX, A, B.

Kamooalii, Kapapala, Kau   HV-210
  At approximately 1,000 ft. elevation, on trail from
  Kapapala toward Puna, near Kamooalii *heiau.*
  Human figures (many variations)—dots—circles—
  abstract shapes.
  Several hundred (one in *heiau* wall).
  Baker (1922), pp. 49–52 (illus.).
  Jaggar (1921), pp. 129–130 (illus.).
  Emory, Ladd, Soehren (1965), p. 83. Pl. 10A, B.

Kahue Inland, Puna   HV-211
  Approximately 2 miles inland from sea, in center
  of *ahupua'a,* in shallow valley.
  Human figures.
  Emory, Ladd, Soehren (1965), p. 88.

kaha" Cave, Panau-iki, Puna   HV-212
   ½ mile east of Panau-nui boundary, near shore,
   on *pahoehoe* dome near cave shelter.
   Human figures.
   Emory, Ladd, Soehren (1965), p. 88.

loa, Panau-nui, Puna   HV-225
   On upper trail from Kealakomo to Kalapana, ½ mile
   N.W. from Chain of Craters-Kalapana road, approxi-
   mately 1½ miles from shore, low *pahoehoe* hill.
   Holes—dots—circles—abstract shapes—a few
   human figures (triangular)—sails—2 capes—*piko*
   ceremony.
   Possibly ±15,000 units.
   Baker (1931).
   Beckwith. ms. B.P.B.M.
   Emory, Cox, and Others (1959), pp. 56, 95, 117.
   Emory, Ladd, Soehren (1965), pp. 5-10.

ue Upland, Puna   HV-233, 235
   Between Holei Pali and Poliokeawe Pali.
   233.   Just east of large lava tube.
          Lineal and triangular human figures.
   235.   Petroglyphs within and outside of house
          enclosure.
          Lineal and triangular figures.
   ±25 units.
   Emory, Ladd, Soehren (1965), Part II, p. 2 (base map).

ua Inland, Apua, Puna   HV-237
   A shelter cave on the east side of a small *aa* flow
   3 miles inland, about the center of the *ahupua'a,* one
   mile east of Keauhou-Apua boundary.
   Several lineal figures on walls of cave.
   Smart. Field notes. Volcano Report.

hue Inland, Puna   HV-244
   Approximately 2½ miles from shore, below Holei
   Pali, ½ mile west of Kahue-Kealakomo boundary,
   collapsed lava bubble. Petroglyphs on rim.
   Several.
   Emory, Ladd, Soehren (1965), (Map X), Part II, p. 3.

alakomo Waena, Kealakomo, Puna   HV-245
   Cave, approximately 2 miles north from shore,
   below Holei Pali. ¼ mile west of Kealakomo-Panau-
   nui boundary.
   Several, on slabs of a paved area.
   Emory, Ladd, Soehren (1965), Part II, p. 3. Pl. 1A.

Niheu's Footprint, Poupou, Puna   HV-297
   On coastal trail from *mauka* side of Wahaula *heiau*
   to Kamoamoa ¼ mile west of Kailiili village.
   Footprint—dots—human figure.
   5 units.
   Stokes (1910), p. 278.
   Emory, Cox, and Others (1959), pp. 48, 49, 82.

Kailiili, Poupou, Puna   HV-298
   In Kailiili village ruins ¼ mile south of Wahaula
   heiau.
   Papamu—meander lines.
   2 only.
   Emory, Cox, and Others (1959), p. 80. Map II B.

Kamoamoa, Puna   HV-300
   On slanting slabs of *pahoehoe* along trail at western
   edge of Kamoamoa village ruin.
   Human figures.
   ±20 units.
   Baker (1931).
   Emory, Cox, and Others (1959), pp. 83, 95. Map III B.

Puumanawalea, Laeapuki-Kamoamoa, Puna   HV-323
   On boundary between the two *ahupua'a* on small
   pahoehoe hill ½ mile from shore on coast trail.
   Dots—lines—3 human figures.
   ±150 units.
   Beckwith. Field notes. 1914.
   Emory, Cox, and Others (1959), pp. 91, 117. Map IV A.

Laeapuki, Puna   HV-324, 329
   In Laeapuki village ruins.
   Human figures (triangular)—lettering.
   ±5 units.
   Emory, Cox, and Others (1959), p. 89. Map IV.

Kealakomo, Puna   HV-335-364
   Scattered throughout ruins of Kealakomo village.
   Human figures (lineal, triangular, muscled)—
   67 *papamu.*
   ±190 units.
   Baker (1931).
   Emory, Cox, and Others (1959), pp. 96-105.
   Map VI B-E.

Kamooalii Trail, Kaalaala Makai, Kau   HV-381
   Approximately 2½ miles west of Kamooalii *heiau,*
   near BM 1,249 for 150 ft. along the trail.
   Figures (lineal, and cut out)—dots—circles.
   Baker (1922), p. 50 (illus.).

Kauai

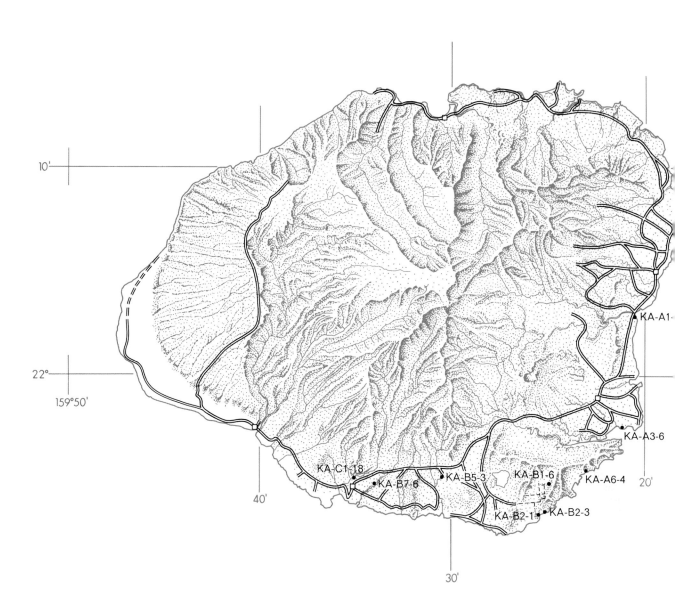

88

Wailua, Lihue   KA-A1-6
    Boulders on shore near the northern boundary of
    Lihue district, south side of mouth of Wailua River.
    Human figures, linear and curved outline—spiral (the
    only one known in the islands).
    ±16 units.
    Dickey (1917).

Papalinahoa, Lihue   KA-A3-6
    Sandstone ledge on north shore of Nawiliwili Harbor.
    Believed destroyed when pier was constructed.
    Human figures.
    ±5 units.
    Bennett (1931), p. 90.

Molehu, Kipukai, Lihue   KA-A6-4
    On limestone beach, approximately ½ mile north
    of Lihue-Koloa boundary.
    Lineal angular human figures, one triangular muscled,
    one curvilinear—circles.
    ±25 units.
    Stokes (1910).

Mahaulepu, Koloa (eastern)   KA-B1-6
    Boulders in cane field approximately 2 miles inland.
    Groove to large cup hole—linear figures.
    ±20 units.
    Kikuchi (1963). (Sites 103, 104).

Keoneloa, Koloa   KA-B2-1
    Beach ledge 25 x 100 feet, sandstone, approximately
    ¾ mile east of Makahuena Point, southernmost tip
    of island.
    Human figures, mostly linear; some are large, some
    ribbed, columnar, triangular—boat (?)—"Lono"
    symbols.
    ±168 units.
    Farley (1898), pp. 119–125.
    Judd (1904), p. 178.
    Stokes. ms. B.P.B.M.
    Bennett (1931), p. 90, Pl. XV (Site 84).

Makawehi Point, Koloa   KA-B2-3
    On sandstone rise approximately ¼ mile east of
    Keoneloa site (B2-1) at east point of bay.
    Geometric grid patterns—lines.
    ±4 units.
    Kikuchi (1963). (Site 101).

Lawai, Koloa   KA-B5-3
    Boulder-cliff outcropping, on James Margus property,
    Iwipoo Rd., Lawai village.
    Linear human figures.
    ±20 units.
    Bennett (1931), p. 90 (Site 71).

Wahiawa, Koloa (Western)   KA-B7-6
    Two areas: Cliff on west side of Wahiawa Stream,
        approximately 2 miles from shore at
        280' elevation.
        On east side of stream (across from
        above) approximately 500' from stream
        bed.
    Linear, angular human figures—lettering—names—
    dates (1883, 1887).
    ±40 units.
    Kikuchi (1963). (Sites 9, 10, 11).

Hanapepe Valley   KA-C1-18
    A small boulder, 1½' x 2½', found by Mr. Nonaka
    on his farm land, in upper Hanapepe Valley, now at
    Mr. Nonaka's home.
    An owl-like "face," pecked.

Fig. 105. Muscled figure
Puako, Hawaii, E3-1 (Kaeo trail)

Lanai

Kahaehole Bay, Kaa   LA-7
>   Largest boulder on north side of valley.
>   Human figures, triangular—rooster—goats.
>   ±15 units.
>   Emory (1924), p. 103.

Panipaa Heiau, Kalulu   LA-49
>   Boulder in south corner of *heiau*.
>   One human figure.
>   Emory (1924), p. 105.

Kalama-iki Bay, Kamoku   LA-71
>   Boulder near stream bed, and a cave shelter
>   near top of north bank.
>   Human figures, linear and triangular—dog.
>   ±5 units.
>   Emory (1924), p. 103.

Kalamanui Valley, Kamoku   LA-72
>   Boulder next to trail where it crosses the stream bed.
>   One human figure, muscled.
>   Emory (1924), p. 103.

Kaumalapau Bay, Kamoku   LA-73
>   Boulder on south bluff of bay.
>   Human figures, triangular.
>   ±7 units.
>   Emory (1924), p. 103.

Keaohia, Kaohai   LA-107
>   Boulder, west of trail in the middle of a hollow in
>   upper Kaohi District.
>   Human figures—dogs.
>   ±17 units.
>   Emory (1924), p. 105. Pl. XI, F.

Kapua Gulch, Kaohai   LA-115
>   Boulders, 200 yards west of gulch, near foot of hill
>   slope, behind stone platform, and west bluff
>   of valley.
>   Human figures.
>   ±7 units.
>   Emory (1924), p. 105.

Awehi Valley, Kaohai   LA-118
>   Boulder, near stream bed at base of west bluff.
>   One human figure.
>   Emory (1924), p. 105.

Lopa, Kaohai   LA-120
>   Boulder, 100 feet toward sea from Haleaha *heiau*.
>   Linear human figures, running.
>   3 units.
>   Emory (1924), p. 105.

Kaunolu Village, Kaunolu   LA-135
>   On boulders, ledge above west side of stream bed,
>   just inland from Halulu *heiau*, 4 areas in 1/2 mile.
>   Human figures, triangular, muscled—goats.
>   ±320 units.
>   Emory (1924), pp. 97–103. Pl. IX, X.

Piliamoe, Kealiaaupuni   LA-165
>   Boulder, several hundred yards S.W. of Luahiwa,
>   on trail S.E. to the coast.
>   Human figures—animals.
>   ±20 units.
>   Emory (1924), p. 103. Pl. XI, B, C, E.

Mamaki Cove, Kealiakapu   LA-173
>   Boulders, on paved trail into cove, and on east
>   bank, several hundred yards from edge of cove.
>   Linear and triangular human figures.
>   Emory (1924), p. 103. Pl. XI, D.

Kuahulua, Kealiakapu   LA-174
>   Boulders on top of west bluff.
>   Triangular human figures.
>   ±13 units.
>   Emory (1924), p. 103.

Luahiwa, Kealiaaupuni, and Kealiakapu   LA-177
>   20 boulders on hillside, west side of Palawai basin.
>   Mostly human figures, linear and triangular—
>   many dogs—horses.
>   ±400 units.
>   Emory (1924), pp. 94–97. Pl. VII, VIII.

Kaimuhoku Village, Mahana   LA-199
>   Boulder, lower margin of village.
>   Human figures.
>   ±5 units.
>   Emory (1924), p. 103.

Poahiwa Valley, Mahana   LA-205
>   Boulder, north side of valley, against house
>   platform, at foot of ridge.
>   Human figures, linear and triangular.
>   ±9 units.
>   Emory (1924), p. 105.

Kukui Point, Mahana   LA-209
>   Boulders, east edge of gulch approximately 200
>   yards from shore, back of signal tower foundation.
>   Human figures—bird-men—dogs—chicken.
>   ±85 units.
>   Cox. B.M. files.

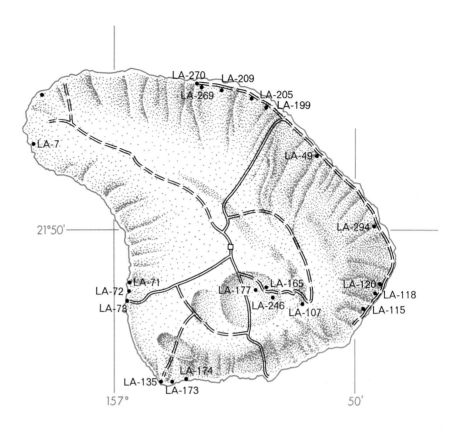

Koi Valley, Palawai   LA-246
>Boulder, south edge of *kukui* grove, mouth of Koi
>valley, and one at very edge of water course, and
>to the south several hundred yards.
>Human figures—dog.
>±15 units.
>Emory (1924), p. 103. Pl. XI, I.

Keonohau Bay, Paomai   LA-269
>Upright boulder, most conspicuous several hundred
>yards back of bay.
>Human figures.
>±5 units.
>Emory (1924), p. 105.

Kahue Valley, Paomai   LA-270
>In four areas within 300 yards of shore on east
>bluff and below.
>Human figures—dogs.
>±27 units.
>Emory (1924), p. 105

Kahea Heiau, Pawili   LA-294
>Boulder in south bank of *heiau*.
>Linear human figures—dogs—pig.
>±20 units.
>Emory (1924), p. 105.

Kaena Point, Kaa   LA-(no number)
>Boulder.
>One human figure.
>Emory (1924), p. 103.

Kapoho Gulch, Kaohai   LA-(no number)
>On cliff-boulder, north side of Kapoho Gulch, about
>200 yards from sea (below and inland from
>Kapoho *heiau*).
>Human figures, triangular with plumed headdresses—
>dogs—two horses—lettering.
>±30 units.
>(Information from E. Stasack. 11/66.)

Maui

Waihonu Gulch, Hana   MA-A16-1
> On cliff face, below Hamoa village, 4 miles south
> of Hana village.
> Pictographs—red paint. Human figures—long torsos.
> Dogs.
> ±20 units.

Maulili, Hana   MA-A24-11
> In Ulupalakua ranch. On cliff 1/3 mile west of
> Kalina Stream. Badly weathered.
> Pictographs—3 figures—red paint.
> Soehren (1963b).

Kaupo Ranch, Hana   MA-A28-1
> On wall of small shelter cave, west of Dwight
> Baldwin's house.
> Pictographs.

Nuu Village, Nuu, Hana   MA-A30-2
> On cliff near shore at Nuu Bay.
> Outlined triangular figures—dogs.
> Painted—±75. Carved—±30.
> Emory (1922).

Papakea, Lualailua Hills, Kahikinui   MA-A37-5
> North of Lualailua hills. On *pahoehoe*—trail, 8 miles
> from Ulupalakua, 13 miles from Kaupo.
> Footprints, 6″ to 10″. 31 prints (10 pairs).
> Emory (1922).

Koheo, Makawao   MA-B16-1
> On cliff face, Koheo side of Kaakaula Gulch,
> above Kula road.
> Lineal figures, crude.
> ±10 units.

Keahuaiwi Gulch, Makawao, Kula   MA-B19-1
> On north side of gulch, ½ mile above Lower
> Kula road.
> Pictographs.
> Lineal human figures—dogs.

Kealahou, Makawao, Kula   MA-B19-2
> On cliff face, in Keahuaiwa Gulch, below Kealahou
> school.
> Lineal human figures—crowded, overlapped.
> ±20–30 units.

Pulehuiki, Makawao   MA-B20-1
> Cliff face, Hapapa Gulch.
> Lineal human figures, multiple limbs—dogs.
> ±60 units.

Kalialinui, Makawao   MA-B22-2
> Cliff face of Kalialinui Gulch, on north and south
> sides, about one mile from lower Kula road.
> Lineal human figures—boxers—canoes (some with
> tassels on sails)—names.

Kaluapulani, Makawao   MA-B23-1
> Cliff face, west side of dry stream bed on down
> side of Waiakoa road, below water tank.
> Human figures—dog—canoes—sails—abstractions.
> ±45 units.

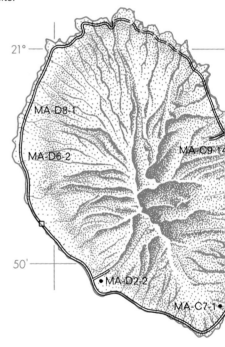

Kuau, Hamakuapoko, Makawao   MA-B26-1
> On large flat rock near ocean, at Kuau Bay.
> Triangular figure—lineal figure—"Lono" (?) symbol.
> ±6 units.

Maalae, Wailuku   MA-C7-1
> Boulders on hillside west of highway, opposite
> Maalae village.
> Lineal human figures—multiple limb figure—
> triangular human figures—circle—dot—dog—goat.
> ±20–30 units.

Waiehu, Wailuku   MA-C9-14
> Boulder in cane field, 2/5 mile due north of Puuohula
> village (plantation camp), ½ mile *mauka* of highway.
> Human figures, triangular bodies—dogs.
> ±60 units.

Olowalu, Lahaina   MA-D2-2
> On cliff face below Kilea hill, on the east side of
> Olowalu gulch, approximately ¾ mile inland from
> the sea.
> Outlined, triangular human figures—dogs—sails—
> letters.
> ±100 units.
> Emory (1922).

Kahoma Valley   MA-D6-2
> On cliff face.
> Figure.
> Newspaper clipping and photo. B.P.B.M.

Honokowai, Lahaina   MA-D8-1
> Large boulder bluff.
> Lineal and triangular human figures—dogs.
> ±35 units.

Keanae Trail   MA- (no number)
> In Haleakala Crater, on trail to Keanae Gap.
> Pictographs.
> Baker (1922), p. 56.
> Emory (1924), p. 94.

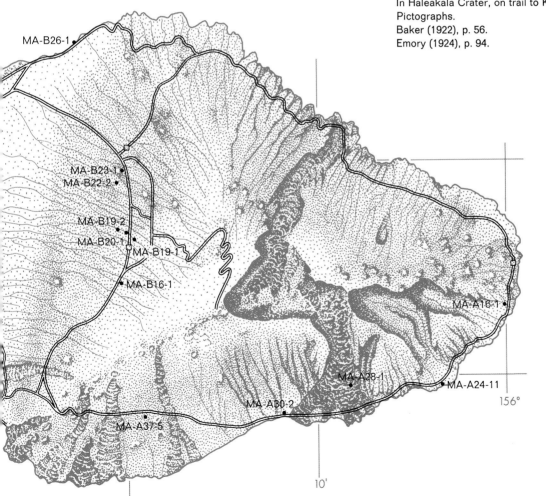

Molokai

Kalae, Palaau 3   MO-2
> North of Kalae. Boulders on top of Puu Lua about
> the middle of the north side of the island. Just east of
> phallic stone (Summers site 1). (Several small stones,
> with markings representing the female organ, were
> removed from this site to the Bishop Museum
> in 1965.)
> Linear human figures.
> ±25 units.
> Judd (1904), pp. 179–194. Stokes (1910), p. 290.
> Summers (1967), (Site 2). Cooke (1949), p. 101
> (photo.).

Kipu Ruins, Kipu   MO-9
> On upright stones lining the inner wall of structure
> "E," southern part of northeast wall.
> Stone apparently removed prior to 1952.
> 2 human figures.
> Summers (1967). (Site 9).

Moomomi, Kaluakoi   MO-25
> In sandstone, near trail ½ mile from sea and
> 1½ miles from Moomomi Bay.
> Footprints.
> ±500 units (Stokes).
> Judd (1904), p. 185.
> Stokes (1910), p. 286 (illus.).
> Summers (1967), (Site 25).

Puu Hakina, Kaluakoi   MO-68
> Three boulders on top of low rocky hill.
> Southwest corner of island, 2 miles N.W. of Hale o
> Lono. Now destroyed (according to Summers).
> Human figures.
> Stokes (1910), p. 284 (illus.).
> Summers (1967), (Site 68).

Kaluakoi   MO-81
> On a large boulder, at the base of the bluff, north of
> road just west of Bench Mark 7, ½ mile east of
> Kukuku Gulch. (Also some reported to the northwest
> of this boulder).
> 1 linear human figure 20" high.
> Summers (1967). (Site 81).

Naiwa 1   MO-106
> On large weathered boulder on slight rise of the
> broad ridge.
> Linear human figures, 8-12".
> ±12 units.
> Summers (1967). (Site 106).

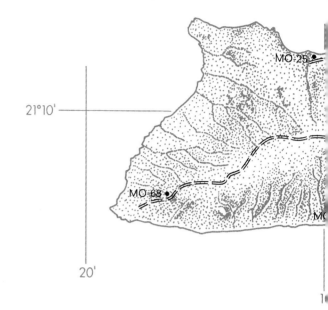

21°10'

20'

Waihi Gulch, Kalamaula   MO-125
> On large boulder on west side of gulch, *mauka* of
> forest fence about 6' above stream bed.
> 4 linear human figures.
> Cooke (1949), p. 101.

Kawela   MO-141
> A boulder with figures on east and north sides.
> South of site 140 (Summers).
> 2 triangular human figures.
> Summers (1967), (Site 141).

Wailau Trail, Wailau   MO-275
> A stone at a place called Pohakuahaka, ". . . at
> the 2750 foot level on the Wailua side of the cliffs"
> (Summers, 1967).
> Summers (1967), (Site 275).
> Described by George Kane (1912), *Ka Nupepa Kuokoa*
> Aug. 2 and 9.

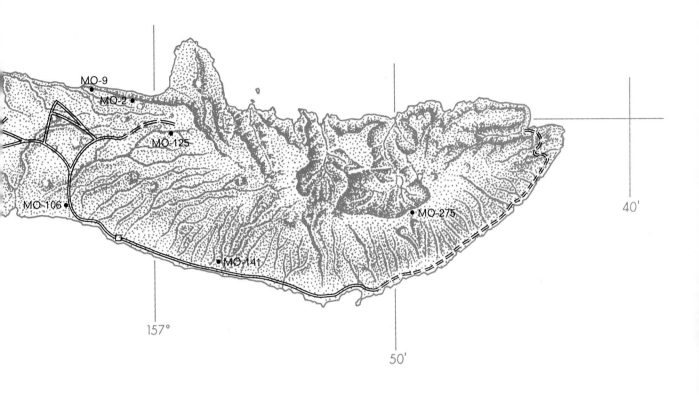

MO-9

MO-2

MO-125

MO-106

MO-275

MO-141

157°

50'

40'

Fig. 106. Figure, symbols
Puuloa, Hawaii, HV-225

Oahu

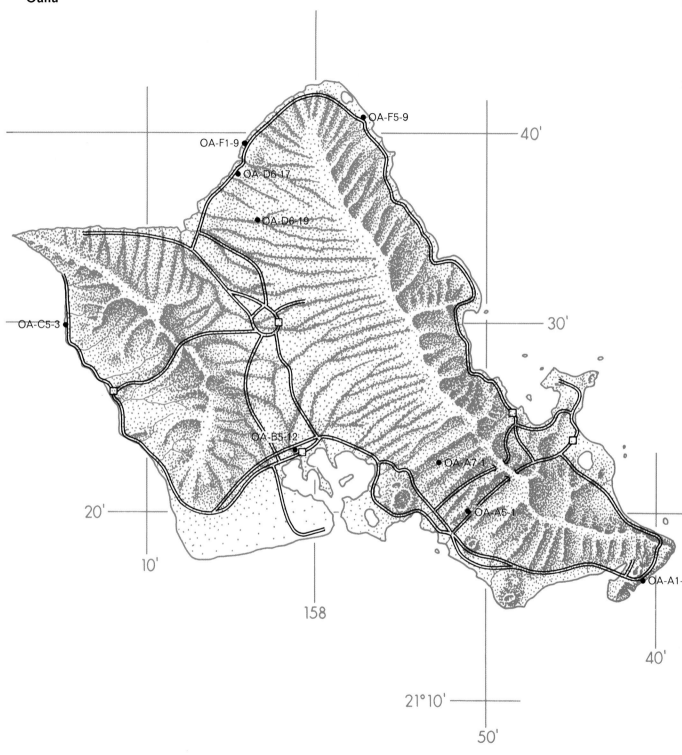

OA-F5-9

OA-F1-9

OA-D6-17

OA-D6-19

40'

OA-C5-3

30'

OA-B5-12

OA-A7-1

OA-A5-1

20'

10'

OA-A1-

158

21°10'

40'

50'

Koko Head   OA-A1-46
    In low slanting cave shelter, at foot of cliff between
    Hanauma Bay and Blow Hole. Sandstone.
    Linear human figures, triangular and columnar—
    sail—dog.
    ±37 units.
    Thrum (1900), pp. 126–128.
    Judd (1904). Baker (1922).
    McAllister (1933), p. 67, Fig. 24 (Site 44).
    Emory (1955), pp. 9–11, 26.

Nuuanu Valley   OA-A5-1
    Three areas: On cliff, west side of Nuuanu Stream,
            at Nuuanu Memorial Park.
            50 feet south of Alapena Pool, west
            bank, in cave-like shelter.
            West bank of Alapena Pool.
    Linear and triangular, muscled human figures—dogs.
    ±40 units.
    McAllister (1933), pp. 83, 84. Pl. 10, A, B; Fig. 26
    (Sites 67, 68, 69).
    Johnson (1952), pp. 20, 21. (illus.).
    Cummings (1955). (illus.).
    Emory (1955), pp. 9–11, 26. (illus.).
    Charlot (1956), pp. 26–29. (illus.).

Moanalua   OA-A7-1
    Boulder by the side of Moanalua Stream on land
    known as Kahalelauki.
    Human figures, linear and triangular—papamu—
    meander lines.
    ±70 units. Many indistinct.
    B.P.B.M. Directors Report (1907), pp. 32–33, Fig. 1–2.
    McAllister (1933), p. 100, Fig. 31, Pl. 10, C-F.
    (Site 93.).

Waikele, Ewa   OA-B5-12
    Cliff boulders, north side of Waikele Stream, west
    edge of Waipahu town.
    Human figures, triangular (arms curved downward)
    —dogs.
    ±12 units.

Keaau, Waianae   OA-C5-3
    Sandstone ledge, south end of Keaau Park, opposite
    first large bridge, on beach. (Sometimes under sand.)
    Human figures, open body deeply carved—dog.
    ±5 units.

Kawailoa, Waimea   OA-D6-17
    On basalt outcropping, on bluff behind #61-264 Kam.
    Highway (Paul Crook's residence). 2/5 mile south of
    Kupopolo Heiau (D6-12).
    Triangular human figures—dogs.
    ±6 units.
    B.P.B.M. Field Book #1. pp. 153–154.

Kawailoa Gulch, Kawailoa, Waialua   OA-D6-19
    Above the opening of a shelter cave (D6-14) on the
    north side of Anahulu River, Kawailoa Gulch,
    approximately 2 miles from the sea at 400 feet
    elevation. 600 feet down stream from siphon
    (flume across stream).
    3 human figures, triangular, filled.
    2 dogs.

Kahuku, Keana, Koolauloa   OA-F5-9
    Boulder on beach.
    1 human figure.

Pupukea, Koolauloa   OA-F1-9
    Sandstone ledge north of Kalunawaikaala Stream,
    at sea level.
    Sunset Beach. (Usually under sand.)
    Human figures—dogs.
    ±70 units.

Lualualei, Waianae   OA-
    Sandstone slab (removed to Bishop Museum).
    Human figure.

References Cited

Fig. 107. Fisherman
Kaupulehu, Hawaii, D22-19

Apple, Russell A.
    1965   *Trails*. B. P. Bishop Mus. Spec. Pub. 53, Honolulu.
Baker, Albert S.
    1919   "More Petroglyphs." *Hawaiian Annual for 1919,*
            pp. 131–135.
    1920   "Still More Petroglyphs." *Hawaiian Annual for 1920*
            pp. 49–52.
    1922   "Petroglyphs from Ka'u." *Hawaiian Annual for 1922*
            pp. 49–58.
    1931   "Puna Petroglyphs." *Hawaiian Annual for 1931,*
            pp. 62–67.
Beckwith, Martha W.
    [n.d.] Field Notes. Hawaiian Sources Collection,
            pp. 384–397. B. P. Bishop Mus. Dept. Anthropology,
            Honolulu.
Bennett, W. C.
    1931   *Archaeology of Kauai*. B. P. Bishop Mus. Bull. 80.
            Honolulu.
B. P. Bishop Museum Department of Anthropology
    1964   Report of the Puako Petroglyph Field in the Proposed
            State Historic Petroglyph Park, Puako, South Kohala.
            B. P. Bishop Mus., Honolulu. Typescript.
Bryan, E. H., Jr.
    1951   "Hawaii's Trailside Picture Rocks." *Honolulu*
            Advertiser Hawaiian Weekly, May 20, pp. 8–9.
Buck, Peter H.
    1957   *Arts and Crafts of Hawaii*. B. P. Bishop Mus. Spec.
            Pub. 45. Honolulu.
Charlot, Jean
    1956   "Post Cook Discoveries in Petroglyphs." *Paradise of*
            the Pacific 68(11):26-29. (Holiday ed., 1957.)
Cooke, George Paul
    1949   *Moolelo o Molokai: A Ranch Story of Molokai*.
            Honolulu: Star-Bulletin.
Cummings, Margaret K.
    1955   "Stories in Stone." *Honolulu Advertiser Hawaiian*
            Weekly, January 16.
Dickey, Lyle A.
    1917   "Stories of Wailua, Kauai." *Hawaiian Historical*
            Society Report for 1916, pp. 14–36.
Ellis, William
    1842   *Polynesian Researches* . . . Vol. 4. 2nd ed.
            London: Fisher, Son, and Jackson
    1917   *Narrative of a Tour Through Hawaii*. Honolulu:
            Hawaiian Gazette.

mory, Kenneth P.
 1922 Rock Carvings and Paintings of Kaupo, Maui.
   B. P. Bishop Mus., Honolulu. Manuscript.
 1924 *The Island of Lanai.* B. P. Bishop Mus. Bull. 12.
   Honolulu.
 1933 *Stone Remains in the Society Islands.*
   B. P. Bishop Mus. Bull. 116. Honolulu.
 1951 "Ancient Carving is Discovered on Kauai."
   Honolulu Advertiser, October 21, p. 1.
 1955 "Oahu's Fascinating Petroglyphs." *Paradise of the*
   Pacific 67(5):9–11, 26.
 1956a "Acres of Petroglyphs." *Honolulu Advertiser*
   Hawaiian Weekly, January 22, p. 3.
 1956b "Kilalowe Was Here, Generation After Generation."
   Paradise of the Pacific 68(3):9–11.

mory, Kenneth P., J. Halley Cox, William J. Bonk,
Yosihiko H. Sinoto, and Dorothy B. Barrère
 1959 Natural and Cultural History Report on the
   Kalapana Extension of the Hawaii National Park.
   Vol. 1. Cultural History Report, pp. 95, 117–120.
   B. P. Bishop Mus., Honolulu. Typescript.

mory, Kenneth P., Edmund J. Ladd, and Lloyd J. Soehren
 1965 Additional Sites, Test Excavations and Petroglyphs.
   The Archaelogical Resources of Hawaii Volcanoes
   National Park. Part 3, pp. 5–10. B. P. Bishop Mus.,
   Honolulu. Typescript.

mory, Kenneth P., and Lloyd J. Soehren
 1961 Archaeological and Historical Survey of Honokohau
   Area, North Kona, Hawaii, pp. 10, 12, 18.
   B. P. Bishop Mus., Honolulu. Typescript.

arley, J. K.
 1898 "The Pictured Ledge of Kauai." *Hawaiian Annual for*
   1898, pp. 119–125.

ornander, Abraham
 1880 *An Account of the Polynesian Race: Its Origins and*
   Migrations. . . . London: Trubner.

iedion, S.
 1962 *The Eternal Present: The Beginnings of Art.*
   New York.

udson, Alfred E.
 [n.d.] Archaeology of East Hawaii. B. P. Bishop Mus.,
   Honolulu. Manuscript.

aggar, Thomas A.
 1921 "Ancient Rock Pictures." *Monthly Bull. Hawaiian*
   Volcano Observatory 9(8):129–130.

Jarves, J. J.
 1843. *History of Hawaii or the Sandwich Islands.*
   London: Moxon.

Jelliffe, Derrick B.
 1963 Personal Communication, September, 1963.
   University College, Makerere, Uganda.

Johnson, Walter R.
 1952 "Stone Age Art in Hawaii." *Paradise of the Pacific*
   64(11):30–31.

Judd, A. F.
 1904 "Rock Carvings of Hawaii: Some Possible Tracing of
   Prehistoric Hawaiians." *Hawaiian Annual for 1904,*
   pp. 179–194.

Kamakau, Samuel M.
 1964 *Ka Po'e Kahiko: The People of Old.*
   B. P. Bishop Mus. Spec. Pub. 51. Honolulu.

Kikuchi, William K.
 1963 Archaeological Survey and Excavations on the Island
   of Kauai, Kona District, Hawaiian Islands.
   Committee for the Preservation of Hawaiian Culture.
   Honolulu. Typescript.

Kuykendall, Ralph S.
 1938 *The Hawaiian Kingdom 1778–1854.* Honolulu:
   Univ. Hawaii Press.

Lyman, Chester Smith
 1924 *Around the Horn to the Sandwich Islands and*
   California—1845–1850. New Haven.

McAllister, J. Gilbert
 1933 *Archaeology of Oahu.* B. P. Bishop Mus. Bull. 104.
   Honolulu.

Malo, David
 1951 *Hawaiian Antiquities.* B. P. Bishop Mus. Spec. Pub. 2.
   2nd ed. Honolulu.

Mathison, Gilbert F.
 1825 *Narrative of a Visit to Brazil, Chile, Peru and the*
   Sandwich Islands, 1821–1822. London: King.

Pukui, Mary Kawena
 1942 "Hawaiian Beliefs and Customs During Birth,
   Infancy and Childhood." *B. P. Bishop Mus. Occ. Pap.*
   16(17):356–381. Honolulu.

Pukui, Mary Kawena, and Samuel H. Elbert
 1957 *Hawaiian-English Dictionary.* Honolulu: Univ. Hawaii
   Press.

Schmitt, Robert C.
 1965 "Population Characteristics of Hawaii, 1778–1850."
   Hawaii Historical Rev. 1(11):199–211.

Smart, Colin D.

    1965   The Archaeological Resources of the Hawaii
            Volcanoes National Park. Part 1. An Archaeological
            Survey of Parts of Hawaii Volcanoes National Park,
            Hawaii. B. P. Bishop Mus., Honolulu. Typescript.

Soehren, Lloyd J.

    1963a Archaeology and History in Kaupulehu and
            Makalawena, Kona, Hawaii, pp. 28, 30.
            B. P. Bishop Mus., Honolulu. Typescript.

    1963b An Archaeological Survey of a Portion of East Maui,
            Hawaii, p. 71. B. P. Bishop Mus., Honolulu.
            Typescript.

Soehren, Lloyd J., and T. Stell Newman

    1968   *Archaeology of Kealakekua Bay*. Spec. Rep.,
            Dept. Anthropology, Bishop Mus., and Dept.
            Anthropology, Univ. Hawaii.

Stokes, John F. G.

    [n.d.] Field Notes. B. P. Bishop Mus. Department of
            Anthropology, Honolulu. Manuscript.

    1908   "Stone Sculpturing in Relief from the Hawaiian
            Islands." *B. P. Bishop Mus. Occ. Pap.* 4(2):31–42.
            Honolulu.

    1910   "Notes on Hawaiian Petroglyphs."
            B. P. Bishop Mus. Occ. Pap. 4(4):33–71. Honolulu.

Summers, Catherine C.

    1967   Archaeological Sites, Molokai. B. P. Bishop Mus.,
            Honolulu. Manuscript.

Thrum, T. G.

    1900   "Interesting Hawaiian Discoveries, More Picture
            Rocks." *Hawaiian Annual for 1900*, pp. 126–128.

Touhy, Donald R.

    1965   Salvage Excavations at City of Refuge National
            Historical Park, Honaunau, Kona, Hawaii, p. 24,
            Pl. 7–18. B. P. Bishop Mus. Dept. Anthropology.
            Typescript.

Westervelt, W. D.

    1906   "Picture Rocks of Naalehu." *Hawaiian Annual for
            1906*, pp. 164–169.

Wise, John H.

    1965   "The History of Land Ownership in Hawaii."
            In E. S. C. Handy, and Others, *Ancient Hawaiian
            Civilization*, pp. 81–93. Rutland, Vermont;
            Tokyo: Charles E. Tuttle Co.

Photo Credits

B. P. Bishop Museum: 9, 36
Norman Carlson: 10, 11
J. Halley Cox: 5, 14, 32, 47, 58, 60, 70, 72, 81, 100
T. A. Jaggar: 35
Kenneth P. Emory: 6, 7
Violet Hansen: 21
Yosihiko Sinoto: 67
Edward Stasack: 1, 2, 3, 4, 15, 43, 82, 84
J. F. G. Stokes: 8